JUST GO WITH IT

JUST

HOW TO NAVIGATE

GO

THE UPS AND DOWNS OF

WITH

ENTREPRENEURSHIP

IT

MANDY GILBERT

LIONCREST
PUBLISHING

JUST GO WITH IT

How to Navigate the Ups and Downs of Entrepreneurship

ISBN   978-1-5445-1433-8 *Hardcover*

      978-1-5445-1431-4 *Paperback*

      978-1-5445-1432-1 *Ebook*

TO MY INCREDIBLE SONS, ISAAC AND SAM

CONTENTS

INTRODUCTION

WHERE WILL YOUR ENTREPRENEURIAL JOURNEY TAKE YOU?

This book shares my journey as an entrepreneur from the early days of my first business, Creative Niche, to the founding of an international design and tech school, and everything in between. Woven throughout my story are all the real-world, hard-earned lessons I discovered along the way. These are the lessons we entrepreneurs don't know we need to know when we're first getting started, and the ones we don't like to share with others when we learn them (because they're just too painful!). And, of course, they are the ones we often don't recognize or even expect to appear, until it's too late.

All entrepreneurial journeys have similarities, but in the end, they are all different from any other, and mine is no exception. I started my business with an $8,000 personal bank loan and a blurred blueprint for success. I wasn't a computer science wunderkind that raised a ton of capital, accompanied by a trusted board of advisors and investors to help guide me every step of the way.

I bootstrapped my business from the ground up, and I wrote this book to share my experience with entrepreneurs who have a vision, limited resources, and a pile of energy. This book is for all those small-to-medium sized entrepreneurial companies that aren't making headlines but are driving economic development through job creation.

It's for the entrepreneur who started a strategic HR consulting company and wants to get out of day-to-day execution and scale their business. For the one who quit their safe office job to pursue their dream of making the best biscotti there is to buy. The one who is taking over a family business and is feeling stuck on how to turn it around. And it's for the 100,000 entrepreneurs in Canada and the 1.5 million in the United States, who start new businesses every year. It is for YOU.

Know in advance that while my experience may help you along the way, I don't have all the answers. Some lessons you'll have to learn yourself, and sometimes more than once. Just like there is no playbook in life, there isn't one for business either. It's your job to learn how to manage both, how to be accountable, and how to lead in good times and bad. Figuring things out on your own takes courage and tenacity—but don't worry, luckily that's what entrepreneurs do best!

None of this is going to be easy. Entrepreneurship demands that we take enormous risks, put ourselves out there, and be vulnerable every day, no matter what the outcome is or how we're feeling. But also, it will be the most incredibly rewarding experience of your life.

We're about ready to get started, but before we do, I just have one question for you:

How do you spend your time when you're at work?

It's okay if you aren't proud of your answers, and it's also okay if you aren't sure how you should be spending your time. That's why you're here.

Just know that as your business changes, so must you, along with the role you play within it. In order to remain effective as an entrepreneur, it's important to always look for new ways to keep your business moving forward—and to keep searching for the most effective use of your time.

The path might not always be linear. In fact, there will be times when it feels like you're constantly backtracking just to keep your business afloat. Other times, it might feel like you're stuck, unable to make any progress at all.

Whenever that happens, here's my best advice and the approach that has kept me sane and successful after all these years: Just go with it.

As long as you are committed to your success, willing to rely on others, and ready to learn, the path forward will eventually present itself.

IT STARTS WITH YOU

During coaching sessions and speaking engagements, I ask the entrepreneurs I am working with or speaking to the same question I asked you: "How do you spend your time when you're at work?"

Often, the answers are pretty vague, something along the lines of, "I'm not sure, I don't know, just a lot of stuff, I guess, mostly planning."

If you cringed a little reading the above, then you're probably thinking the same thing I do every time I hear it: "That entrepreneur has no idea what they're doing!"

Of course, whether we like to admit it or not, that's the reality for many of us—especially in the early going. We get an idea we're convinced could change the world, we set up a business to make that idea a reality, enjoy some early success, and then we stall out.

There are plenty of perfectly reasonable explanations for this. After all, entrepreneurs have a particular personality. We're easily excited and easily spurred to action. When we get a good idea, we tend to leap before we look. That is, we're usually already in the thick of things before we've fully thought out our plan—and then before the dust settles and we have time to regroup, we're off chasing down some other crazy idea.

This mad-scientist-like energy is what makes us so wonderful. But when left unchecked, it's also what makes us frustrating to the rest of our team, especially after we've grown our business and we have employees to look after.

It can be hard for us to admit it sometimes, but many entrepreneurs don't know the value we're supposed to be providing to our companies. We don't know what our own job is—and therefore, we don't know how to effectively lead, manage, and grow a company.

But here's the good news: that same mad-scientist energy that got you this far can be harnessed. As an entrepreneur, you already have all the qualities you need to become a dynamic, effective leader. All you need is a nudge in the right direction.

There are very few easy wins in business. The line between struggling and thriving, between success and failure, is often razor-thin. Having a good idea, then, isn't enough.

The entrepreneurs who succeed are the ones out there on the front lines every day, looking for ways to move the needle for their business. They're taking care of their teams and initiating strategic projects that will benefit their organization, making everyone more successful and more efficient.

Entrepreneurs like this have one thing in common. They know the business they create is the result of the precedent they set.

If you're content simply to survive, to pay the bills and live a semicomfortable life, then that's the business you will create. However, if you're dead-set on thriving, if you lie awake at night wondering how you can grow your business into something meaningful, then that will be the business you create.

Now, tell me, which business would you prefer?

If you picked up this book, then no doubt you want the latter. Once upon a time, when I was an eager twenty-something looking to break out of my nine-to-five and chart my own path, that's what I wanted, too. And over the next decade-and-a-half, I fought tooth and nail to make that dream a reality. Today, three businesses and a lot of investments later, I'm proud to say I've made it.

My path to success wasn't easy. Like many entrepreneurs, I was full of ambition but low on practical experience when I first set out on my own. All I knew was that I had a vision for something different and a passion to make it happen. As the years unfolded, I got a lot of things right and a lot of things wrong, but either way, I emerged a little wiser for the experience. Of all the lessons I've learned, perhaps the biggest one is that you can't go it alone.

Being a leader means showing your team you have their backs, that you're always going to be on the front lines fighting for them, and you're working hard to lift them up alongside you so that you can celebrate the wins (and, yes, commiserate the losses) together.

However, being a leader also means knowing when to ask for help. It means identifying what you're best at and then finding the most talented people on your team to do the rest. It also means trusting your team to be your filter when you're firing off too many wild ideas, and it makes taking their feedback seriously, although, at times, it may be painful. Most importantly, it means being proactive about how you spend your time—and making sure you are always adding the most value possible to your business.

In terms of my experiences contained within these pages, I have endeavoured to fully disclose situations as they occurred with no sugarcoating. Likewise, this book isn't a how-to manual, although it offers a lot of suggestions. Rather, it is my entrepreneurial biography and is filled with many of the events that led me to where I am now.

It has been an incredible developmental journey with significant emotional experiences, and trust me, it will be the same for you. Just go with it.

CHAPTER 1

GETTING STARTED

WHAT BROUGHT YOU TO THE THRESHOLD OF BECOMING AN ENTREPRENEUR?

I suspect there are as many pathways to becoming an entrepreneur as there are entrepreneurs. Regardless of what brought you here today, your entrepreneurial journey has started, and you are on your way to achieving the success you have envisioned and deserve. My journey has been a unique process with lots of twists and turns that have taken me to the brink of despair one day and incredible heights the next. Glean as much as you can from my experiences to maximize the potential of your journey—and don't forget to enjoy yourself!

MY FIRST STEP

After two years of working in specialized recruiting, where

I played matchmaker for clients and candidates, I'd been asked to help a multinational open its operations in Toronto, Canada. I was super excited, a little bit mystified, and completely unsure of what I was supposed to be doing. So there I was at twenty-five, a manager in charge of five employees with the responsibility to build a new division for a public company.

And my training? "All right, get after it."

That didn't seem to matter to my director. After his sparse words of encouragement, he smiled and walked away, leaving me at my desk with little clue of what to do and a whole lot of questions.

But, if my only marching orders were to get after it, then that was exactly what my team and I were going to do. I began by setting up a basic two-step strategy:

1. Sell, sell, sell.
2. Deliver excellence without exception.

It didn't amount to much, but it spoke to our position as the new kid on the block. As a startup expanding into a new marketplace, we needed to be aggressive with our large-client acquisition right out of the gate. Further, if we were going to keep those clients and gain some traction, we needed to do things the right way.

Miraculously, our two-point plan worked. Soon, our Toronto office was the most successful in the company, even competing head-to-head with both the New York and LA markets. For the next two years, we enjoyed nonstop growth.

As our startup grew, so did my responsibilities and skills. First, the company began flying me out to California to sit on one of its committees. Then, before I knew it, I was being introduced not only to the various members of the C-Suite, but also to the chairman of the board.

That's when they dropped the bombshell. "We want to offer you a new position," they said. "We still need to write the job description, but once we do, we'll send that along with our formal offer."

It arrived the next week, and it was certainly generous. Not only would I be making tons more money—a $60,000 boost to my base salary, plus a huge variable component—I would also get to travel to our other branches to help them get established in new markets.

My jaw hit the floor. A huge pay bump and the chance to rack up those airline miles? To my twenty-seven-year-old mind, it all sounded too good to be true. As it turned out, I was right.

SECOND THOUGHTS

As excited as I was by the opportunity, my gut was telling me something wasn't right. The feeling began when they asked me to sign the offer, then and there, which struck me as odd. I stalled, asking if I could take the night to go home and think about it. The entire ride home, I kept asking myself over and over: *do I want this?*

Every fibre of my being screamed *no*, yet I didn't understand why.

My husband didn't understand either. Newly married, we were young, ambitious, and ready to build our careers and start a family. To him, the opportunity was a slam dunk. "The pay boost alone is reason to go for it," he said. "Why would you turn it down? Because of the travel?"

It wasn't the travel—at least, not directly. The truth was, while I enjoyed my success at the company over the past couple of years, I wasn't exactly thrilled with the company itself. I enjoyed recruiting, but I didn't believe in my company's approach, which was formula-driven. It was a numbers game. My team and I were expected to make an outrageous number of cold calls each week and interview as many people as we could.

This unrealistic workload told me my company didn't care much about its employees, nor did it care about delivering the best results for its clients. All it cared about was its bottom line—which was quite healthy—and it pit salespeople against each other to reach it. This, of course, led to remarkably high turnover. So many people were coming and going that they had to change the key code to get into the office each week!

I had succeeded there, but I had no illusions about the kind of company I worked for, but now that I had a chance to rise up the ranks, it was a time of reckoning.

If *I* didn't believe in our company and its process, how could I travel around the United States and preach it to others? Besides, promotion or not, did I *really* have any job security in that kind of environment?

But there was more to the story—though it took me years to understand or admit it.

AFRAID TO SPEAK UP

During my time at the company, I was often the only woman at the table and surrounded by a ton of men. This in itself wasn't a problem, as I have no problem hanging out with the right group of guys, but the men at the table were not them. Being the only woman in the room at a company with a toxic culture and an outdated view of women is something entirely different. Some of my male colleagues simply didn't know how to make room for a woman's voice at the conference table.

I was often afraid to speak up—and when I did, my voice would literally become a liability. I have a young-sounding voice. It's no big deal to me, but especially when I was younger, every time I would speak up in meetings, one of two things would happen: one of the men in the room would say, "Oh, listen to her cute voice. Mandy, you're so cute." Or, I'd start to speak, and then someone else would talk over me, rolling up my suggestion into his, as if he were the one who had thought of it all along.

In both cases, their behaviour was unprofessional and insulting.

I'd like to say that was the worst of my treatment, but sadly that's not the case. There were many instances when leadership and coworkers would cross the line, saying wildly inappropriate things, making passes, and even groping me.

I'm not naïve. I knew that behaviour like this from anyone was inappropriate. But, like many women then and now, especially young professionals, I didn't have the confidence to say anything. I never reported any of this behaviour because I thought no one would believe me. Even now, reporting sexual harassment can put a woman at risk of losing her job. In the early 2000s, it was all but guaranteed.

If I had reported what I'd experienced, I would almost certainly have been accused of lying or seeking attention, and I didn't want to be fired for someone else's inappropriate behaviour.

Instead, I did what many young women do in similar situations: I locked the experiences away in a box and didn't think much about them for years. Only my sister knew what had happened. Of course, denying these experiences doesn't make them go away. That growing pit in my stomach wasn't just about taking a promotion with a company I didn't truly believe in. It was also the dread of knowing that if I took the job, I would be subjecting myself to similar treatment for years to come. I wouldn't fully understand this feeling until several years later, but it was there just the same, and I knew I couldn't ignore it.

The next day, after a long night of soul-searching, I signed the contract—and then walked over to the nearest paper shredder and destroyed it.

These days, when I hear stories of women coming forward decades later with their own stories of harassment, I understand. When you're a young woman, and all you're trying to do is make your way, it can be hard to understand what has happened to you, and even harder to say anything about it.

ON MY OWN—AND LOVING IT

The moment I shredded that contract, I knew that my time with the company was over. It was time for me to set out on my own. But before I told them as much, I needed to lay the groundwork for my next steps. So, I took a half-day, headed off to the bank, and asked for a line of credit.

I'd been doing well the past few years, but my husband and I had just spent all our money on our wedding. We had no savings and no assets to leverage for a small business loan.

Instead, I just said we were planning to upgrade our furniture and needed a little help. The second the bank approved me for an $8,000 line of credit, I walked into my old office and resigned.

I started my own recruiting company, Creative Niche, the next day.

At this point, it was 2002. I was still young, and I had plenty of options in front of me. I could have gone back to school and pursued a career in another sector, or I could have taken my experience in the industry and found a similar job with another company. Neither option sounded appealing. I was too invested in the recruiting world to change careers, but I was also tired of putting up with the winner-take-all, revolving door culture of my previous employers.

I liked what I did, but I didn't want to do it for other people anymore—and I now had the skills to do it myself. Besides, I'd always wanted to become an entrepreneur, and my husband and I were living a modest, kid-free lifestyle at the time. The timing was right to realize the dream of becoming an entrepreneur.

I envisioned Creative Niche as a specialized recruitment company focusing on marketing, digital, design, and advertising. We would work with companies of all shapes and sizes, from Fortune 500s to New York banks, mutual fund companies, and advertising agencies. Whenever they needed to hire an intermediate to senior-level candidate, whether part-time or full-time, they would hire us to help them find that person.

It wasn't going to be easy, though. Although I'd been in the industry for years, I would be starting from scratch. My former employer had asked me to sign a non-solicitation clause back when I started, which meant I would have to completely rebuild my base of clients and candidates.

The temptation to call some of my old contacts was certainly there, but I took my legal obligations seriously and wanted to do things the right way. If I was going to make Creative Niche work, I was going to have to get after it. Fortunately, I had a strong background in sales to help me get up and running.

For the next several months, it was hustle, hustle, hustle, sell, sell, sell. Wherever I could, I asked people for referrals and told them that if I could place their friends with a client, then I would reward them with a cash incentive.

I'll never forget my first placement. After meeting with a prospective client earlier in the day, I received a call a few hours later. "We're going to go with you. We need a graphic designer for two weeks," the client said.

More firsts soon followed. My favourite came when our first contractor faxed over his first time sheet. I was so excited that I promptly framed it and hung it on the wall. Just like that, I was in business—meeting with promising candidates, connecting them with new clients, and growing my small operation.

At this point, I was excited to be getting work, but still broke and living off a furniture loan. Even so, I had enough self-awareness to know that I needed a real office. If I worked from home, I knew I'd get stuck in a rut. Plus, a big part of my job was meeting with clients and candidates, and I thought it would be weird if I had to keep doing that at a coffee shop.

I found a small co-working space in the heart of the advertising and design community in Toronto. I had about 150 square feet to myself, where I set up a desk and an old-school, big-bubble purple iMac (which I loved). I had a little space to store my bike but no natural light. It wasn't glamorous, but it was *my* office, and I'll always remember it fondly.

"Splurging" on the office meant I didn't have much cash for anything else. Aside from the furniture loan, I had otherwise refused to ask anyone for money. To keep my expenses low, I rode my bike to the office and packed my lunch every day.

I had no margin for error, and it was exhilarating. I thrived on the challenge of having to make more money before the loan money ran out. Every morning, I woke up dying to start the day. I'd get to work around seven, and often I wouldn't leave until nine or ten that night. At one point, I was down to only about three weeks' worth of money, but rather than panic, I just put my head down and got after it.

Week in, week out, this was my routine, and I *loved* it.

Sometimes when I told friends and family about my typical day, they didn't understand. They said it sounded miserable—all work and no reward. But I felt free. Prior to founding Creative Niche, I had spent years in a micromanaged, untrusting, fear-based culture. But now, I no longer had anyone looking over my shoulder telling me what to do and how I should do it. I got to figure things out on my own.

Granted, there was a lot to figure out, but it never felt overwhelming. Working hard wasn't new to me. Working long hours wasn't new to me. But being in charge of my own destiny was. It was up to me to keep myself alive and to pay the next month's bills. At first, I was barely making enough money for any of those things—but I had never felt so alive.

MAKE YOUR OWN WAY

I've spoken with enough entrepreneurs over the years to know that many of our stories have a lot in common. Sure, the details are different, but the broad strokes are the same: we weren't happy with the direction our careers were going, we weren't happy with the work culture we saw around us, and we had a better idea of how things could be done, so we set out on our own.

The result is a time in your life that is both incredibly liberating and incredibly vulnerable. On the one hand, you're thrilled at the prospect of being able to call your own shots. On the other, you're acutely aware that it's all on you. If you're not willing to put your head down and do what it takes to build your business, then your journey may be over before it starts.

Still, there's a huge upside to be in a position of such vulnerability. When your only options are to go for it or to quit, you gain a tremendous sense of clarity as to what needs to be done. There's no time for strategy, no time for planning. There's only enough time to execute on the two fundamental elements of business: (1) sell, sell, sell, and (2) deliver excellence without exception.

I was acutely aware of this during those long, early days in my tiny, windowless office. I knew that if Creative Niche was going to survive, I had to do all the right things—building relationships, being nice, being proactive, asking for business, and getting in front of clients wherever possible.

It worked, and just six months later, Creative Niche had done well enough that I was able to hire my first employee. I was thrilled, but there was a flurry of new questions. What kind of boss was I going to be? What kind of culture would I create in my company? What would we stand for? How would I make sure that employees felt safe and inspired?

I didn't have the answers, but I knew I wanted to create an environment where my employees could grow both as professionals and as people. Further, I wanted to create a culture that didn't normalize the kind of gendered double-standards and sexual harassment that I'd experienced at my previous company. And this went double for our clients: under no circumstances would we work with assholes.

Most importantly, though, we'd be a company of people who embraced being an underdog, willing to put our necks on the line and just go with it. We would succeed by making our own way. Now came the hard part: putting that vision in writing—and recruiting the kinds of people who could make it a reality. How hard could that be?

CHAPTER 2

BUILDING THE FOUNDATION

WE'VE GOT A COMPANY

When I was making enough money to keep the lights on, it was time to hire my first employee, which meant it was time to shift my mindset from solopreneur to employer. This represented a brand-new challenge for me. At the time, I was still only twenty-seven, with little in the way of managerial experience. I knew exactly what kind of employer I *didn't* want to be, thanks to my previous job experiences, but I'd never been in a position to set the company culture and organize a workforce on my own. That time was now!

One thing I knew for certain: even though Creative Niche was in its startup stage, I wanted my employees, right from the get-go, to feel like they were working for an established company. In my sector, employees at established companies had variable compensation packages on top of their base salary. My goal from day one was to exceed earning potential and perks, and it is something I revisit regularly.

In my eyes, that "real company" vibe would be vital to attracting and retaining talent, and the only way to bring great people on board was for Creative Niche to be a great company. If new employees felt like they were taking a step back or losing something by joining a small business, then it would be an uphill battle to engage and retain them. I wanted my future team to feel confident that they would have the same support and opportunities available at a large company—perhaps even more since my team would be coming in on the ground-floor level with wide-open potential for future consideration.

I decided the only way to attract high-calibre employees from day one was to show them I was serious about their future, and to achieve that, I needed to write a company handbook.

REAL COMPANIES NEED REAL HANDBOOKS

A lot of small businesses have neither the time nor the inclination to write a company handbook. A startup may have a loosely defined set of company policies, guidelines, and perks, but more often than not, they aren't formalized and therefore, there is little or no accountability to abide by them.

Not us. I wanted to make sure that we were forthright with our candidates and our community and that we walked the talk right from the very beginning.

Creative Niche was going to have a comprehensive employee handbook beginning with our very first hire. This handbook would detail everything we stood for—our core values, dress code, and expectations around acceptable behaviour. Not only was this just good policy and provided some legal context to the business, it also protected the employee and client experience.

Now all I had to do was find the time and energy to write the darn thing.

I was in full entrepreneur mode before I knew it, so to save time, I read every employee handbook I could get my hands on and researched them meticulously. I even bought a template as a guideline, which I kept open at all times. In the evenings, I would tackle one section at a time in a massive mind dump, covering everything I could think of under the sun, including, but not limited to, the following:

- Mission and values
- Attitudes (i.e., how we show up for work)
- Hours of operation
- Learning allowance
- Anti-discrimination

- Sexual harassment
- Community hours (Nichers Give Back)
- Paid holidays and vacations
- Dress code
- Computer and equipment usage policies
- Working remotely

I included anything and everything I thought might help to guide or mitigate negative employee conversations down the road. If I didn't feel like I nailed a section on the first try, I would revisit it again when inspiration struck.

But I didn't stop there. From the early going, I was a big believer in transparency. So, in addition to spelling out what I expected of them, I also included a section that covered what was expected of *me*.

Finally, I hired an employment lawyer for about $700 to help with all the legal aspects of the handbook. After writing the letter of employment, I worked with a benefits provider and added this information to the finished handbook. And that was it. We were set up and ready to rock and roll.

If you're getting to the stage of hiring your first employee, here are some key features I would recommend you include in your handbook.

EXPECTATIONS

The handbook began with our offer letter of employment, along with our mission, vision, and corporate structure. Everything was broken down by position so that every person who came on board knew they were joining a serious and legit company and understood what was required of them to be successful.

By so doing, not only do your employees get a better idea of what it takes to be successful, but so do you. I found it essential in understanding who would succeed and who wouldn't. For instance: You have an employee who isn't meeting your identified targets or KPIs. When you approach them to discuss it, they indicate they were never trained on what was required to be done every day in order to be successful. If you haven't defined these expectations in your handbook, job description, or letter of employment, your employee would be absolutely right.

One's perception of success is entirely subjective, but if you've provided a proper and thorough on-boarding process that explains what is required and what success looks like, the likelihood your staff will achieve success is much higher.

But the problems don't stop there. Now you're stuck wondering whether the employee *can* be successful given the right training. However, when you establish an operational foundation of expectations—and reinforce it often—you take second-guessing out of the equation, and it will be much easier to build a successful business.

LEARNING ALLOWANCE

I wholeheartedly believe that if you provide relevant and competent training, team support, and hire the right people—there's no reason they will not be successful. In fact, I provided a learning/professional development allowance of $800 a year to my very first employee.

You may think a learning allowance might feel like an extravagant expense for a startup operation. Why would I spend $800 a year on helping my employees learn when it wasn't guaranteed that I'd even be around in a year?

The answer was easy for me: Creative Niche puts people first, and so should you.

I built in a learning allowance for my employees because I wanted them to succeed, and I knew if they succeeded, so would the company. Although I recognized that I was driven enough to succeed in the recruitment sector and start my own business, I wanted to attract people to my company who were smarter than me. I wanted them to feel appreciated and supported as people and professionals, and feel invested and engaged in the company's purpose and long-term growth.

I've seen plenty of entrepreneurs who don't operate with this mindset, and statistics prove they are shooting themselves in the foot. You can see it in their attrition numbers and feel it when you step into their offices.

In the years since implementing a learning allowance, I've learned that one of the biggest challenges is getting your employees to use it. My recommendation is to do whatever you can to encourage them to take advantage of this opportunity. A workforce that is learning and developing is a workforce that's engaged and successful. For that reason alone, the education allowance is well worth the investment.

WORK FROM HOME

The office at Creative Niche is made up predominantly of women, some of which are mothers with young children. They spend forty minutes in the morning getting ready—feeding their kids, getting them into snowsuits (it gets cold in Toronto!), getting them into the car, and shuffling them off to day care. *Then* they have to trek into the office by car, train, or bike, or sometimes even on foot. I asked myself: "If I can trust people and give them permission to work from home two days a week, what might that concession do for their life, and how will it impact our culture?"

The option to work from home wasn't in our original handbook. However, in the years since writing it, the nature of

work has evolved (and will continue to do so), and we exper-
imented to see how offering such a perk would impact our
communication, collaboration culture, and bottom line. We
tested the process for a good six months, and the results
shocked us: everyone's performance actually *improved* by
working from home!

There are other benefits as well:

- There is no additional cost to the company.
- Telecommuting is better for the environment.
- It supports the emotional well-being of the staff.
- It allows employees to take longer lunches in order to
  get a workout in, rest, go for a walk, do some laundry,
  or even start dinner.

Once we saw the boost our work-from-home policy was
giving us, we rolled out the program company-wide—and
we haven't had one regret.

While we love being flexible with our work-from-home
policy, we've also found that it's good to set a few healthy
boundaries. On Mondays, for instance, we require everyone
to be in the office. We have also established mandatory
happy hours and company meetings once a month at the
office.

When the COVID-19 pandemic hit, we were ahead of the

curve, and it didn't negatively impact our operations, culture, or ability to service our clients.

IT ALL COMES DOWN TO ONE QUESTION

Would you want to work for your company?

I get a lot of interesting responses from other entrepreneurs when I ask this question. Some are an enthusiastic "Yes!" Others quickly blurt out, "God, no!" Still, others aren't sure how to answer the question. They've never thought about it before. If you aren't sure, try these questions instead:

- Does everyone know what success looks like for them and how it contributes to the company's vision and goals?
- Do you acknowledge your team and individuals in big and small ways?
- Do you offer flexibility and perks to make their lives and time with you more enjoyable?
- Do you ask your team how your company could be better?
- Do you reward people for achieving various results?
- Do you help your staff develop so they can achieve success?
- Do you fire toxic people?
- Are you providing training and experience to enable staff to be promoted?
- Are your employees having fun?

What do you think now? Is the picture getting any clearer? I'll give you a hint: if you answered "no" more than you answered "yes," then you probably wouldn't want to work for your own company.

Remember, no matter what stage of development your business is operating at, your employees' work-life balance is in your control. If you want, you can create a work environment that outcompetes the big companies and draws all the top talent. Sure, the big companies offer interesting amenities, perhaps, but with a little imagination, you can as well—it's not as expensive as you think! Besides, the possibility exists that you can offer something larger companies can't: a unique employment experience.

This is the number one opportunity that many entrepreneurs don't realize they have when it comes to recruiting and sustaining key employees. Being smaller in size can be an advantage to your company, not a disadvantage. Small businesses are nimble, while big companies are inflexible. You can throw out old policies and procedures and replace them with something else tomorrow if you want to. The big companies would have to analyze and test potential changes to death first, especially since one tiny modification can impact so many employees.

But you have to be purposeful, and you must be willing to look at things differently. Most importantly, you have to be honest about what is and isn't working in terms of your leadership style.

Here are a few things to help you hold yourself accountable.

TRUST

Many old-school business types don't trust their employees to work from home. It provides them with peace of mind to watch their employees in order to make sure they are working. But here's the thing: if you have the right people, they'll get the work done no matter where they're doing it from. If you *don't*, then do you really think they're getting any work done even when they are in the office?

If you have the wrong people, you have the wrong people. And if you have the wrong people, then you have a hiring and firing problem. It doesn't matter where they work. The results will be the same.

Of course, working from home is just one issue, but it's a great example of how trust works. Many large companies don't trust their employees to manage themselves. That's their loss. You'll attract far more talent if the policies and guidelines in your handbook demonstrate trust.

If that's going to be a problem for you, here's my suggestion: take the leap. You'll never learn to trust your employees if you don't take a chance. Whatever guidelines and structure you need to include, go for it.

Every action creates a reaction, and sometimes they are extremely positive, as has been the case with our work-from-home policy. Since we had implemented that policy years ahead of the COVID-19 pandemic, which forced companies and government agencies to adopt work-from-home opportunities for employees, Creative Niche didn't skip a beat. Staff was already accustomed to working virtually and were able to carry on their daily routines.

It is interesting how innovations that benefit employees are becoming the norm as opposed to the exception, as leaders have been forced to think about the future of work now.

COMMUNICATION

Sure, you know what your company does because you started it. But how you experience your business and how your employees experience it are two very different perspectives. To get a sense of your employee experience, it's good to audit yourself from time to time, from job postings to your on-boarding process.

Here are some questions to consider:

- What technology are you using?

- What are you doing to motivate your staff every day?
- How are you communicating?
- Are you being transparent about where the business is and what the financials are?
- Are you connecting with every role or department so that staff know their contribution to the overall strategic plan?

Everyone wants to contribute, but in many companies, employees don't know how because the company is keeping it a secret. They don't even know what the overall goals of the company are—and if they don't know what they are, how can they do their best work? How can they even understand what they're supposed to be doing?

When you build a magical culture with high levels of engagement and everyone is accountable for their success and subsequently the success of the company, the team learns how to succeed, and they are acknowledged for it. That's the magic.

Plus, it takes the pressure off you. I don't always have to be the smartest person in the room. In fact, I like it when I'm not. But I do prefer to be in a room where everybody trusts each other. Like any entrepreneur, I tend to get fired up about certain things, and that attitude creates a healthy tension. Because we're focused on culture, my team knows exactly how to respond to me, sometimes by pushing back and other times by having a good laugh. In an environment filled with strategy, transparency, and trust, good things can and will happen.

If you can connect all these dots for your employees, then you will build a company that has a strong culture. It's the difference between sliding and expanding and between having stability or always having to drop everything to go and put out fires. The latter is exhausting and a major distraction to any entrepreneur and business.

DON'T HIRE AT A DISCOUNT

During the first decade of development, Creative Niche expanded, contracted, and even experienced an identity crisis, but we survived it all.

The primary reason for our success as a company has been our ability to recruit talented people. Some of that success can be credited to my decision to create our handbook early in the process, along with my commitment to make Creative Niche an attractive and positive place to work and grow. In the process, we learned how to hire for both senior- and junior-level roles to create a balanced workforce focused on growth.

Especially when they're starting out, entrepreneurs tend to go cheap and only hire junior professionals when they build their teams. I was like that too, though I now wish I had hired more senior people out of the gate.

Yes, it's costly to hire senior people, and many entrepreneurs don't think they can afford it—or they think the more experienced prospects won't be interested. So, they turn their attention to more junior-level prospects. They know they're taking a risk with these less-experienced recruits, but they figure they can mould those juniors into what they want. I've found that the pros of hiring more senior-level professionals far outweigh the cons.

If you're a good enough leader to get feedback and be collaborative, then you can absolutely work with senior people. Plus, you can benefit from their wisdom, their expertise, their networks, their calmness under pressure, and their ability to think strategically.

These traits are far more valuable than you might think. Unlike their senior counterparts, junior-level employees are rarely strategic. Due to being inexperienced, they often don't think about why, how, and when. Certainly, it can be good to have a few doers in the mix, but if that's your entire workforce, you're in trouble. If all you have are doers, then you're not growing your business. Senior team members are leaders who can add structure, stability, and vision to your business.

While it's true that some juniors can absolutely be moulded

into your exact vision for them, more often, it's a constant cycle of weathering their mistakes, losing them, and then replacing them. This kills your traction and your ability to execute—which ultimately keeps you tied down by the daily needs of your business.

If you have experienced leaders who are aligned with your vision, key objectives, and way of doing things, you can delegate to them and let them do their jobs. However, if you have juniors running wild, you have to clean up their mistakes and micromanage them, which greatly reduces your time and ability to think strategically.

Build your A-team from the beginning. Focus on quality over quantity. Hire people you can't afford. A cheap and cheerful staff might seem nice, but they will almost always cost you more in the long-term. You're better off hiring senior people who are still willing to roll up their sleeves and get some work done.

These are the kinds of team members who already know how to steer the ship and are accountable for their actions. If you share your vision, conduct yourself in a professional manner, and provide your team with clarity on what is required to be successful for them personally—as well as for the company—you will create a solid foundation upon which to build a sustainable and profitable future.

SET THE TONE EARLY

When I wrote the handbook, I had no idea its value would penetrate to the inner core of every single aspect of my company's operations. Without a doubt, the handbook and its outreach influence have been the most important tools used in the development of my company. Most entrepreneurs don't write one until they've already taken on several employees—if they write one at all. If you don't take the time to produce a company handbook, you're going to be fighting fires constantly, and if that has been your experience, you know how exhausting it is to be in that situation.

Now with public access and visibility into your company through anonymous review and rating websites, it is even more important to ensure you are on top of your employer brand and employee experience. Low star ratings and negative comments can spook potential A-players and target candidates. It's hard to attract great people when you've got retention issues.

As more millennials move into the workforce—and with Generation Z nipping at their heels—employee handbooks will only become more important in the future. This isn't because younger generations are lazy and entitled (I am *so* sick of people saying that). It's because they want to be treated with respect and want clarity. Keep in mind, if the turnover rate among millennials is higher than it is with other generations, then it's because their leadership isn't engaging with them.

Here's the bottom line: it doesn't matter which generation your employees belong to. If you don't engage with them, they're going to leave.

But, while the generational conversation is overblown, I will suggest that it does help to design your handbook with them in mind. If you do, you'll find that you are satisfying every generation. A forty-five-year-old will appreciate the flexibility to work from home. A forty-five-year-old will also appreciate having a clear picture of what success looks like for them and being acknowledged for their contribution. A forty-five-year-old will also appreciate knowing how to advance their career and have opportunities to learn and volunteer. The generation doesn't matter. In my experience, what millennials want, everybody wants.

EARLY INVESTMENT, LONG-STANDING PRECEDENT

As an entrepreneur, I have had to grow and develop myself. I've had to build and scale my business and move it into new sectors. I want to have people on my team who believe in our brand and what has been built, and who will help to expand it further.

Has my leadership been perfect in this regard? Absolutely

not. I've made mistakes. I'd even say I was a disaster for a while, but one thing I did right from the outset was committing to being generous with and trusting my employees. That commitment has never wavered. In fact, the further along I get in my journey, the more I focus on creating a meaningful employee experience.

I'm glad I got this part right. As a result, my first hire turned out to be a slam dunk. For the next two years, she and I made a lot of progress working out of our 150-square-foot office. I would handle sales and payroll, and she focused on recruiting. I would get the business, and she developed our candidate roster. Later on, I hired another salesperson and then another recruiter. Eventually, I hired a senior person, had some attrition, and then the company started to really take off.

Today, our company handbook is still very similar to the original document of seventeen years ago. We have updated our core values and policies, and we've loosened up our dress code. We have also changed our employee benefits and the way we work. Every year, I send it to our lawyer to update legal aspects to reflect changing workplace laws. Things change—I am always looking at what we can do as a company to provide a modern way of working—but the core of that document hasn't changed.

Of course, even the best handbook is worthless if you don't

use it. We refer back to ours constantly, setting the tone during on-boarding. Every new hire has to read it and sign an acknowledgment they have done so. Through every chapter of our story, it's been an invaluable tool.

Ultimately the initial investment in learning and creating a company culture of engagement, respect, and open communication, along with the development of our company handbook, have resulted in an average employee tenure of about eight years. We are proud to say it's one of the best in the industry.

The more employees work with others, build relationships, and gain knowledge, the stronger our culture and the more stable our business becomes as a result. And the more stability we have, the more freedom I have to focus my energy on growing the business.

CHAPTER 3

FROM ENTREPRENEUR TO... PARENTREPRENEUR

STRATEGIC, INTUITIVE, OR IMPULSIVE

By early 2005, the company had moved into an office with about 1,000 square feet of space. It was definitely a step up from the 150 square feet I shared with my first employee, but now at four employees, we were filling the space fast.

At one end of the office, there was a little meeting room where we met to discuss strategy, hold staff meetings, and entertain clients. Outside of that, we had enough space for a few desks. We still had no kitchen, so we had to wash our coffee mugs and lunch plates in the bathroom. I remember thinking I would love to have just a little more space to not feel so cramped. As luck would have it, I was about to get the extra space—and a whole lot more, since I was now three months pregnant.

One day, I bumped into my property manager in the elevator. As if he could read my mind, he asked me if I was looking to move my company into a larger space. He explained that another company in the building had recently folded, and its 3,000-square-foot space was open for the taking—along with all the beautiful Herman Miller furniture the company was willing to sell at a discount.

We went to have a look at the office; I took it on the spot.

At first, I thought it was an impulsive move; I had no idea how this expansion was going to fit in with the rest of our plans. I just knew we had to get out of our old space, and I was confident I would be able to increase business enough to justify the move.

In a fifteen-minute time span, I had committed to a workspace that was three times what we currently had, and no one on my team even knew what had happened!

That was the next order of business. Excitedly, I went back to my office and told the team we would be moving upstairs—immediately.

Then, I told them that we were going to spend the next six

months—prior to my maternity leave—filling our new space with awesome colleagues. It was time to go big or go home.

Unsurprisingly, the staff had questions. They were unsure about my desire to get bigger. All of them had left big companies to come work for me, and they didn't want to end up in an inefficient bureaucracy again.

I did my best to reassure them. "We're going to grow this business, and we're going to have a lot of fun in the process. It doesn't mean we are going to work long hours; we're going to work smart and be damn good at what we do. We're going to fill this office up as we develop our careers, and in the end, feel super proud of what we've built."

They weren't fully sold, but they were willing to go along with it for now. So, I marched them up to the new office and told them to take their pick of all the gorgeous window desks that were available. You could almost see their minds turn a corner in that moment. Suddenly, they were all in.

For the next few months, we wore our mission to fit into the new space on our sleeves. It became a major talking point among both candidates and clients. Everyone became excited about this challenge, and they were all rooting for us.

It worked. We added three new employees in just three months, which is significant for a small business, especially when you consider we were doubling our workforce from a few weeks ago. By the time I went on maternity leave, we were up to seven employees, filling out our new space nicely. I'd made a big decision, and luckily it paid off. Was it strategic, intuitive, or impulsive…and did it matter?

THE ZOMBIE BOSS

I loved the company I had built so much, but I also knew I was going to love my baby even more.

I was right. Being a new mom was amazing, though I didn't anticipate how difficult and demanding it would be. You can accomplish nothing in a single day and still wind up exhausted—all because this adorable and precious little person has you running everywhere, doing everything, while they are trying to figure out their new world.

Naturally, my perpetual entrepreneur brain made things more difficult than they had to be, as just two days after my baby was born, there I was in the office, trying to get things done. I was already missing the social aspect of work and wanted to feel the buzz and the energy of the office. Besides, newborns sleep a lot. I should be able to get plenty of work done, right? Of course not!

The baby wasn't the only one who needed to sleep; I did too. I wouldn't admit it to anyone, but I was a zombie, shambling around the office, barely aware of where I was or what I was doing.

It wasn't just because I missed the thrill of the office. I'd had a blast spending the past six months growing our business and filling our new space with bodies. But in all the fun, I'd forgotten to off-board my responsibilities to anyone else. My baby had been born, but I had no one to step in and be me. So, I figured I'd do it myself.

I struggled like this for two months before it hit me: my son was only going to be this young once; it was my first time being a mother—and I *wanted* my maternity leave. If I was going to transition from entrepreneur to parentrepreneur, then I needed to find a mini-me, someone who could take over and keep the company rolling while I enjoyed some much-needed time off.

Luckily, it didn't take long to find my replacement. I reached out to a former associate, someone who had trained me in the industry years earlier and who had evolved in his own career in the meantime. He had a great reputation in the industry—but most importantly, I trusted him and felt confident the team would respect him.

Soon, we were meeting for coffee. I asked if he would be interested in joining my company as president, he enthusiastically agreed, and I committed to him on the spot. Then, for the next four months, I disconnected from my business and connected with my baby.

It turns out I was really good at maternity leave. I loved it. But by the time my son was six months old, I suspected it was time to go back to work. Actually, it was pretty obvious. One day, my husband came home from work, but before he could hang up his keys or take off his coat, I was in attack mode. I demanded that he come into the kitchen and explain how his process for loading the dishwasher made any sense.

After a few tense moments of silence, I snapped out of my bloodlust. "I think it's time to go back to work," I said.

"Yeah, I think so," my husband agreed with an awkward laugh. "I'm going crazy."

WHOSE COMPANY IS THIS?

The initial plan was to go back to work part-time, working about three-and-a-half days a week at the office. But a lot had changed in the four months I was gone. Our new president had changed things up so much, I could barely recognize my own company.

He hadn't done anything wrong. Actually, he had done a lot of good things. The company was just different now. He had restructured the business so that everyone reported directly to him, and he had developed a certain direction and plan for where the company was going. Further, he had made several of his own hires. The team was now up to twenty people, and there were a lot of faces I didn't recognize—and likewise, they had no idea who I was in the scheme of things.

What got me the most, however, was the culture shift. The whole office put out a different vibe now. Our open-concept office may have been full, but everything was quieter and more down to business. I sat at my desk next to the president and barely talked. Because he was a quiet worker, I became one too.

In some ways, changes like these were to be expected. I had been gone for four months, after all, and I didn't expect him to manage the same way I did. I had hired him to do a job, and I trusted him to do it—even though I was aware at the time that I would do things differently.

That whole first week, however, all I could think was, *Oh, no. What have I done?*

It wasn't hard to figure out why my return had felt like such a shock. When I brought on my replacement and shifted into mom mode, I hadn't fully thought things through. I hadn't considered what it meant that I was replacing myself. I hadn't considered that I would be coming back to a different company. And worst of all, I hadn't considered that

I wouldn't be getting my old job back—a job that I now realized I sorely missed.

I tried to put a positive spin on my new role in the company. On the one hand, it was nice not having to run the company. Let the pressure be on someone else for once. But on the other hand, I didn't know what my job was anymore, and no longer knew how to contribute to my own company. For the next several weeks, I puttered around trying to be useful where I could, but I still wasn't sure what I wanted to do in my new role—or what that new role even was.

An opportunity soon presented itself. One of my rock star senior employees approached me and said she wanted to move to Ottawa. She expressed her love for the company, but she wanted to be near her support system. I believed in her (I still do), and I didn't want to lose her, so I decided we wouldn't. Creative Niche would open a new office for her to manage in Ottawa, and I would drive the effort.

It didn't take long to sell her house in Toronto and buy a new home in Ottawa. During that time, we found the perfect office space to expand the business into the nation's capital. I did everything I could to help set it up. I painted, I bought and assembled the furniture from IKEA, I set up the phone line and the Wi-Fi, and so on. Within two weeks, our Ottawa branch was ready to go—and I am thrilled to say it is still going strong today.

Opening the Ottawa office taught me how to be comfortable in my new role—and how to let my business develop without micromanaging everything. I could step up and get things done on special projects like the Ottawa office, and I could also step back, let our president do his thing, and trust that he would continue to do a good job. By 2008, Creative Niche was doing about $6 million in sales and had grown to twenty-three employees.

Happy with the direction in which the company was headed, I decided I didn't want my kids to be too far apart in age and planned for baby number two.

This time, though, I wanted to make sure I wouldn't be missed and that our president had all the support he needed. It was time to bring in a general manager, and I already had just the right person in mind: a client who had worked in a similar role at an ad agency. I knew she would work well in parallel with our president and directly with our teams, providing support and tech updates and making sure everyone was working as efficiently as possible. Now our president could go out and focus on new business development and contribute to expanding top- and bottom-line results.

I had my second child in May of that year, and this time, I stayed home from day one, confident that everything was well under control.

WORK-LIFE BALANCE—DON'T IGNORE IT

When I first became pregnant, I had two employees and was just starting to grow our business. Then I got the wild idea to move into a new space and fill it with new employees.

Looking back, I can't believe I got it all done. I must have really believed in myself.

At least, I believed in the other things I wanted for my life. I knew I wanted to have a family, and I wasn't going to put that on hold. It didn't matter that my business was at a crucial point in its growth. It didn't matter that we didn't have much money in the bank. It didn't even matter that our one-bedroom apartment was decidedly not kid-friendly. I knew what I wanted, and I knew I could figure out how to make it happen.

And that's exactly what I did. Even with my second child and the stormy clouds of a recession on the horizon (which is a story we'll get into later), I made it work.

If I learned one thing during those years, it's that you can't put your life on hold.

Many entrepreneurs struggle with this. They keep putting off important life decisions until the "right time" comes along. But there's no such thing as the right time. If you put your life on hold waiting for that perfect moment to come along, then you'll never start your business, buy your first home, or, in my case, have children.

Is it hard to transition from entrepreneur to parentrepreneur to entrepreneur? Absolutely. If that's a path you're considering, know that some days aren't pretty. I remember one time, I got stuck in a meeting and was late coming home. On the way, the nanny called to let me know that she'd run out of milk, and my son wasn't accepting formula. I was so distracted by the sound of him crying in the background and the guilt I felt that I ran a red light. It was nuts, but thankfully it also made me realize that something had to change. If I kept trying to do it all, I might literally kill myself.

I get why it can be hard for entrepreneurs to let go of the reins and let someone else take over. In a way, your business is like your baby; you give life to it, nurture it, and later struggle with it as you watch it grow. On the other hand, it is important to remember that you built this business so you could call your own shots and enjoy your life, not to be a prisoner of it. If you *are* going to start enjoying life, then eventually, you're going to have to make some different decisions and surrender a little control.

CHAPTER 4

MAKING IT WORK

MY FIRST INTERVENTION

Upon arriving at the office one day, three key team members pulled me into the boardroom, closed the door, and asked me to sit down, all the while staring at me in the most serious way. I had no idea what was going on and was becoming anxious—they had an envelope prepared for me—and even a witness to observe the proceedings! If I were an employee, I would have thought I was getting fired.

Oh no, I said to myself. *It's a mass exodus; my whole team is quitting and abandoning me.*

It began, "Mandy, you know we love you and the company, but we feel we have to speak out and bring some unpleasant things to your attention, not to offend you, but to clear the air so we can all move forward together."

"Oh, damn, what did I do now?"

"You've been getting into a lot of trouble lately, missing meetings and being disrespectful of everyone's time by being late for appointments. But that's not all; you have been overly ambitious with your calendar, to the point none of us can book any time with you because you are always double-booked. You schedule flights for the wrong date, and you don't allow for realistic travel time between meetings. You're making a ton of mistakes, and it has to end."

"As of today, girl, you have an executive assistant, and it's Jayla!"

They definitely had my attention as my eyes swelled, and then, everyone embraced me.

"You know and trust Jayla. She is a detailed and organized professional. Here is her new job description and a plan for you and her to follow over the next two weeks. We gave her access to your calendar and travel schedule, and we also moved her desk closer to you."

And with that, it was over. I'd just had my first head-on intervention.

The second intervention was to present me with a new handbag, along with a message that rang loud and clear. I've never been a flashy person, preferring to just grab an odd handbag from the mall or wherever. But one day, when I came into work, ahead of an important business trip to New York to meet with CEOs, I was once again called into the boardroom where my team intervened.

"We are becoming a very successful company, and you need to dress accordingly. Please accept this new handbag as a gift from the company. We went to the finance director, and he has approved the purchase of a beautiful, black Louis Vuitton bag we picked out for you that is going to represent your brand better. You cannot continue to walk around with your ugly purses anymore."

So every now and again, I get thrown into the boardroom for an intervention, but I'm so grateful that my team has only done so with the best of intentions—and on both occasions, they were absolutely right.

Back to the first intervention. I needed an EA, and I was thrilled it was going to be Jayla, one of the nicest people you will ever meet. From the first day in her new role, I embraced her as my right-hand woman, and I know I'd be lost without her today, all these years later. She keeps me on track both personally and professionally and always looks out for my blind spots.

I thought I'd done reasonably well managing the transition

to parenthood, hiring a president, and carving out my new role in the company. But like many overambitious entrepreneurs, I was constantly finding myself underwater.

Having an EA began the much-needed process of focusing my work, guarding my time, and bringing clarity to my value as the leader of my company.

And if you are asking yourself, "But what about the handbag?" Well, that's a story for another day. Suffice it to say, it is still my favourite, and you can't begin to imagine my swagger of confidence when I walked into that meeting with the CEOs in New York City.

THE VALUE OF AN EA

When I'm at speaking engagements, I often ask how many of the gathered entrepreneurs in the room have EAs. I'm always surprised that, on average, only 5 to 10 percent of them have taken the initiative to hire one. But for those who have ten or more employees, having an executive assistant isn't just a good idea. It's absolutely essential to achieve company goals and objectives and maintain a healthy culture.

If you don't have an EA, everyone around you suffers—but none suffer more than your family and children. Consider for a moment everything you need to think about as a parent. There are basketball leagues, playdates, vacation scheduling, hearing tests, vision tests, other related doctor appointments, and so much more. When you are running two businesses, like I was at the time, you need assistance. Otherwise, things *will* get lost in the shuffle.

Jayla has helped me to keep my life on track so I could focus on one priority at a time. When I was with my family, I could focus on family. When I was at work, I could focus on work. Before Jayla, I never wanted to burden people with what I considered to be "my" work. I never wanted to ask anybody for help because it wasn't their job. With Jayla, however, I never felt guilty giving her work because it *was* her job—or it was her job to find someone who could help me when and where required.

One of the biggest objections to hiring an EA is the investment, which, to be sure, *is* significant. Many entrepreneurs would prefer to hire another salesperson rather than an EA, whose job is to make life easier and more efficient for the entrepreneur.

However, that is somewhat shortsighted when you consider your value to the company—which is significantly more than having another salesperson, especially if you have the time to focus on your unique ability. When your EA is handling all your noisy work and you are freed up to do your thing, the value you bring to your company grows exponentially, far more than any salesperson could generate.

SIMPLIFYING THE WORKLOAD

Having an EA also opened my eyes to the wonderful world of delegation. Suddenly I realized I had a lot of responsibilities I didn't want anymore. I also had a lot of people in the company who were not only capable (and better) to take on that work but would be happy to do so. Boom—it was theirs.

I'm not sure I would have learned this lesson without my EA. Entrepreneurs are often hardwired to do everything, which in the end means we don't do anything really well. We'll onboard customers but forget to put a contract in place. These might feel like innocent mistakes, but they're the kind of mistakes that can break you! When you delegate, you not only simplify your workload, but you make sure the person who *should* be doing the work is actually performing that role. And when you can do that, then you position your business to not just survive, but to advance.

Again, a lot of this comes back to trust. If you don't trust people, and you don't put the structures in place to enable you to rely on people within the company, then you'll never free yourself up to enjoy your life—which is precisely why you became an entrepreneur in the first place.

My first maternity leave taught me how hard it was to withdraw from the day-to-day operations of my company, and my second maternity leave reinforced it. But even so, I still found myself slipping back into the same trap of feeling like I had to do everything!

Our company was growing, and I was sharing responsibility for the day-to-day operations, but still, there was always the temptation to lose myself in one project or another.

It wasn't until I started my second major business that I truly learned how to become my best self as an entrepreneur. With two companies and two kids who depended on me, I had no choice but to put leadership structures in place at work and support mutual parenting roles at home. Otherwise, I would go insane.

I wanted to focus on my business when I was at work and focus on my kids when I was at home. Was that too much to ask for myself?

That said, it's important you don't take your support structure for granted. Sometimes when we offload responsibilities to others, we end up with additional free time, and we don't know how to use it. So, we start taking on more responsibility or projects—and suddenly, we're back to having no free time again, and the people we're relying on are also overworked.

It comes down to balance. Just because you have a partner or a team who has your back, it doesn't mean you can take advantage of them. If you do, your business will suffer, your marriage will falter, and you will struggle as a parent. Don't fast-forward your life by ten years and regret not having made memories with your kids. It isn't that you need to go on fancy vacations. Rather, it's just being there with them. When that time is gone, it's gone forever. Don't let yourself miss out on the joy of parenthood or the adventure of being an entrepreneur. With an EA, you can do both.

I'm still working on this, and every year I get better at organizing my time and delegating. Three days a week, I pick up my kids from school, and I spend time with them from four o'clock to ten o'clock. They may play Xbox, and I might veg out or write an email, but we're together during that time. We watch movies, play basketball, and talk, but most importantly, we have fun together. And guess what? My business is doing just fine without me micromanaging it.

PRACTICE SELF-CARE

To recap: if you can't detach yourself from your business, your personal life will suffer. You'll lose friendships, you'll stop going to the gym, you'll forget to make doctor's appointments, your financial health will slip, and you won't be your best self.

That may be fine and dandy if it's just you (not really), but think about the *you* your family gets, your partner gets, your kids get: the person who is stressed out, negative, always staring at a device, always worrying about cash flow, concerned about firing an employee, and not achieving sales targets. Even if you're physically there, you're not *really* there.

You didn't start this business to work *harder* than you've ever worked while making *less* money than you've ever made.

I get it. Especially in the early days of the entrepreneur's life, you feel like everything is an opportunity. You have to say yes to any and all deals that come your way. You feel like you have to get out there and make something happen.

But sometimes you're better off leaving work early and going to the gym. You will have great ideas while working out! You'll feel confident and go home with energy for your family. You don't have to be everywhere. For example, I've restricted lunch meetings to two a week, so I can go to the gym during that time three days a week.

That flexibility is also a cool thing about being an entrepreneur. Since I have made these changes, I am with my family more, I feel healthier than ever before, and my business is growing.

You provide for your employees, so why not provide for yourself and your family? Work from home once or twice a week, go to the gym, take a friend out to lunch, or attend a conference. Ask yourself how you can make the biggest impact while working the least amount of time and without giving up anything. It *is* possible, but you have to do some soul-searching to find it.

FILTER YOUR OPPORTUNITIES

In the early years, when we were having kids and the business was growing, it was easy to be gone all the time. My husband was in sales, but he was home by four every day. Between him and the nanny, I knew someone had my back. I'd often miss dinner because there was no shortage of demands on my time. I'd go give a speech here and go to a networking event there. Then I'd come home and tuck my kids into bed at night.

Before I knew it, I was gone four nights a week.

Once you start speaking or working on the road, people start reaching out with additional opportunities. "Listen, this other event is happening in Berlin. Why don't you come to Berlin? We'll cover your costs." If you let it happen, the dinners, speaking engagements, and conferences will become your norm, so be selective with the opportunities that present themselves to you.

After returning from a trip, I pulled my EA aside and said, "I'm saying yes to way too many things. I don't want to pack my suitcase for a long time. Let's create a scorecard for business travel." I wanted to identify only the travel opportunities that would either make a lot of money, inspire me, or be a crazy amount of fun.

Once the scorecard was developed and in place, I was no longer the victim of my "yes" impulse. I became selective about what opportunities I agreed to—which reduced my travel by 40 percent—and once again, my business kept on growing.

Before accepting invites to dinners, galas, and other events, I ask myself if attending that event is really adding value or whether I'm just experiencing FOMO (fear of missing out). Because if you really want to be home more, go to the gym, and achieve *balance*, then you have to make some decisions regarding your priorities.

Sure, there are still weeks where I'm flat-out, where I have four speaking engagements back to back, and I'm bouncing from airport to airport. In between that, I'll have sales presentations with clients and side projects that have captured my attention.

But during those weeks, every single opportunity was a priority and a valuable use of my time, and I was happy to go all-in for a little bit.

Those periods are exceptions and not my norm. I say no to

half of the events I'm invited to, and for others, I'll ask an employee if they would like to replace me. It's an opportunity to learn something new and have some fun. The irony is that people usually tell me I didn't miss out on anything by skipping some of these events. It's okay to just be happy with FOMO and know that you're going to have it from time to time. At the end of the day, you are in control, and not every opportunity is going to be an amazing result for you.

ARE YOU HAPPY?

If you want to, you can always find something to occupy your time at work to distract you from your life, especially when you're unhappy. Some entrepreneurs like to micromanage their employees to death. Others like to work on the weekends "to make sure we don't fall behind." Many have superhero syndrome; they can't resist the urge to fly in and rescue clients or offices. Some of them rarely take a holiday—or even take an afternoon for themselves—so they can have rest and relaxation time, reenergize, and be with the people they love and care about.

The saving grace for all of us to remember and never forget: it's never too late to stop yourself from going down that path.

Again, life won't wait for everything to calm down at work. The only way to live your life is to live it. If you're worried that you're falling into the perpetual entrepreneur trap,

take a moment to look around. The signs should be obvious—and if they're not, your employees will be happy to
tell you whether you're overworked or ignoring the best
part of your life.

Simply ask yourself, "How can I lighten my load? What can
I take off the shelf and hand to someone else?"

I finally understood how important this was by the time I
had my second son. And I'm glad I did because the world
was about to throw our company into chaos.

CHAPTER 5

CRASH GOES THE ECONOMY

REACTIVE PROACTIVITY

Unfortunately, my maternity leave with my second son came to an end a couple of months after it started. The Great Recession of 2008 was upon us. It was time for me to be back at work if my company was going to survive.

We had no idea how bad it was going to be as the recession slowly infiltrated the company. It started off with a weak August, which was typical as summer came to a close. But then, the September numbers were also in decline—then October's and finally November's.

The irony is, we were thinking the situation wasn't too bad, so for the first thirty to sixty days after coming back, I kept myself to a part-time role, working only one to two days a week. But by month four, I was all-in.

As the holidays approached, we organized our major event of the year: an annual expensive client-appreciation holiday party, combined with a significant donation as we had done in previous years. A week or so later, the bottom fell out of our market. Before the holidays, we were working on finalizing an $800,000 gross profit chunk of business that would have been realized early in the new year (since we operated on a contingency basis, we were only paid for successful results). By January 15, our gross profit had diminished all the way down to $30,000, a 96.5 percent decrease in potential cash flow from what we had to work with just a couple of weeks earlier.

The office was like a morgue, as it was now completely overstaffed. No one had anything to do. My hardest workers all looked like deer in headlights; they were hardwired to do *something*, but whatever that something was, they couldn't find it.

That's when I started to get nervous. Were we going to be okay? As it turned out, not before the situation became a whole lot worse.

In addition to the terminal condition of the economy, we had another money problem. I had been working with the same small business accountant for years. I had always trusted this person, as I had no reason not to, but suddenly his behaviour became increasingly erratic. When he advised me to transfer a huge sum of money into one of my holding companies and informed me we didn't have to pay any taxes, I knew it didn't make sense.

I decided to have another accountant audit his work. Sure enough, he had made significant mistakes in my last four corporate tax returns. When my auditor informed me that in order to straighten everything out, we were looking at about $450,000 in tax penalties and interest, I thought I was going to have a panic attack.

I couldn't believe it—not just the potential penalties, but the incompetence of someone I trusted with my business.

Luckily, I'd always been a little paranoid that something like this might happen, so I had a good chunk of change saved in the bank for a rainy day. (A friend had always told me it was good for entrepreneurs to be a little paranoid— it keeps them on their toes. Turns out, she was right.) I used the savings to clear up the accounting mess and extinguished one financial crisis in the process, but now I was totally vulnerable.

And there was still the matter of our burn rate, the money going out with nothing coming into the company; we burned through over $400,000 in a matter of months. Some of this was inevitable, but if I had reacted faster and begun downsizing the business sooner, the worst of it could have been avoided. Lesson learned!

The reason I didn't react faster was simple: I didn't know what to do—and neither did our president. Neither of us had expected the recession, and both of us thought things would turn around quicker than they did. We argued constantly about whether to let anyone go. He wanted to keep everyone, and I wanted to contract as quickly as possible. He would ask for one more week, then three more weeks, and so on. When it was clear we had to let some people go, he demanded I give the employees better severance pay, even if it would cripple the business.

I understood his position. He was loyal to the people he managed, and I respect that decision. I didn't want to let staff go either, but while we argued, the company was hemorrhaging money. There was no other choice, and eventually, we were reduced to a skeleton staff.

I'm not going to sugarcoat it: getting there was rough and took an emotional toll. Back before the recession, I'd had a professional photographer come in and take photos of all twenty-five employees in the office. We had a big gallery wall, and everyone's photo hung there. It seemed like a great idea, a nice way to showcase our team by including everyone, but I hadn't considered the worst-case scenario. What happened when employees began to leave? I soon found out.

As the downturn worsened, some staff elected to leave, while others had to be let go. Each time, I'd wait a few days and then take their photo off the wall after everyone else had gone home. I didn't like doing it, but it felt distasteful to leave them up.

Soon, my ex-employees' photos had grown into a nice stack on my desk—and the gaps on the wall became a glaring reminder of how bad things had become. By the time we hit rock bottom, only five photos had remained.

Every night as I was getting ready to head out of the office, I stared at them with tears in my eyes. They stared right back—each with the same desperate question burned into their faces:

"What are we going to do now?"

THE FIGHT OF OUR LIVES

As an entrepreneur, when your back is against the wall and your business is on the line, there's only one thing to do: lead by example. Put your head down, and produce.

I moved my desk into the middle of the office, where my

remaining employees worked. Every day, they'd walk in and see me at my desk, making calls. Every day, as they readied to leave, they saw me there, still making calls.

My team members heard every call—and it was painful. Some clients were honest at least and would call to tell us how they had lost their jobs or that they had just let their entire team go. Others would make up the strangest excuses just to avoid the grim reality they were facing, embarrassed because it was happening to them.

The reality is we weren't suffering alone—everyone was in pain.

In such an environment, I wasn't just fighting for business as the leader; I was responsible for creating and maintaining positive morale. If we were going to survive this recession intact, we had to remain positive. I began to look for small ways to lighten the mood in the office. Once a week, for instance, I would splurge and bring in a fruit tray or a plate of cookies, and we would talk about the importance of a positive outlook and focus on business, as well as life in general.

My favourite tactic, however, was the way I made my employees celebrate every small win. I went to a vintage shop, bought everyone their own brass bell, and explained that whenever something positive happened, they were to ring them. They didn't have to close a deal; even if someone just received an email, we'd celebrate. If a company reached out to us because they needed to staff three people, we'd celebrate—and then we'd immediately get to work and get a contract. As long as the win had the potential to be translated into something bigger in the future, we'd celebrate.

Some of my employees today still have their bells. They don't use them, but every now and then, they'll tell people the story, and we all have a laugh.

Although my persistence didn't turn our business around directly, it definitely changed our attitude and outlook. We couldn't control the economy or control the fact that many of our clients were suffering, but we *could* control how we responded to the challenge. We *could* control how we thought and what we did in the office every day. We came to realize there were some companies out there who were still doing well and needed our help. We just had to find out who those companies were and win them over.

Slowly but surely, that's exactly what we did, and eventually, the yearlong onslaught of lost revenues, lost employees, and disappearing clients came to an end, and we recovered.

WALKING THE TALK

I had a shit boss at one of my earlier jobs. He was cold. He they blamed and shamed others for things that weren't their fault, and he didn't contribute anything. If I ever ended up in a management position, I promised myself one thing: not to become that person.

Luckily, that was a low bar to clear. All I had to do was walk the talk and start doing.

Leading by example has been my go-to leadership strategy ever since that realization, especially if I sensed something was amiss in the company culture. My old boss taught me words were meaningless if they weren't backed up by action.

That's why I hit the phones so hard during the recession. If I wanted my employees to find the energy to help save the company, I first had to show that I was prepared to do it myself. I had to embody the energy that I expected to see emanating from them.

None of this was easy, of course. I hadn't done cold-calling in a long time, and I got rejected—a lot. Every time I did, I could see an employee or two snickering at their desk. They liked seeing me humbled, and I understood why. I was getting what I deserved, as far as they were concerned.

They could snicker all they wanted, but I was still going to be there every day from nine to five (and often beyond), cranking out calls. Eventually, I couldn't be ignored. My employees saw that if I was doing it, they should probably be doing it too. So they did.

Leading by example continues to be a fundamental and consistent trait I adopted early in my career as an entrepreneur. I've never seen the value of getting on my high horse and telling someone how things are done. You'll earn a lot more respect—and inspire a lot more action—if you *show* them how it's done first and lead by example.

People want to contribute, be successful, and provide value. It's inherent within our beings to want to make a difference, but oftentimes we just don't know how to do it. In those moments, it's your job and mine, as leaders, to assess the situation, be vulnerable, and show our teams the way forward.

When business picked up, my team didn't expect me to stay on the phone. They were fine with me popping back up and doing the role I knew I needed to do: run a business. Leading by example doesn't mean doing everything for everyone all the time. It just means that when your team needs to throw down and get shit done, you are the first person to enter the fray.

The value of leading by example can't be overstated. It wasn't just therapeutic for my team; it was therapeutic for me as well. As soon as I jumped into the fray, I was able immediately to sleep better at night. Sitting at the desk and cranking out those calls gave me status as a doer—and ultimately, it enabled our business to find its way back from the brink.

One of the big takeaways from that experience—aside from wanting to never find myself in that position again—was the importance of culture. Company culture is not a one-and-done thing. It changes, and you have to stay on top of it. You may not be able to control it, but you can figure out what it needs. If it gets sick, how can you make it better? I was about to learn that sometimes you have to look inward to find the answer.

A MUCH-NEEDED BREATHER

After things were finally back on the right track, I spent a lot of time reflecting on what had happened.

I didn't handle the recession well. I had sleepless night after sleepless night, I was losing my hair, I wasn't talking to my husband about anything, and I constantly worried that my house was at great risk.

Worst of all, I was concerned about my personal value, my self-esteem. *Only losers burn through that much cash*, I told myself. *How could I put myself in this position? What kind of half-ass* entrepreneur *was I anyway?*

Hell no! I was Mandy Effing Gilbert, a kind and generous

person who had built Creative Niche from an $8,000 bank loan into a multimillion-dollar corporation, an impressive achievement by any standard.

That said, I knew I could be better. I'd learned a lot over the past several years, and there was still a great deal I didn't know, though there was one thing of which I was absolutely certain: I never wanted to go through an experience like that again.

It was time to learn how to navigate the future more strategically. It was time for me to have more sustainability as an entrepreneur.

It was time for me to invest in myself.

CHAPTER 6

INVEST IN YOURSELF, INVEST IN YOUR BUSINESS

YOU CAN FOOL SOME PEOPLE SOMETIMES, BUT YOU CAN'T FOOL YOURSELF

Although I don't have an undergraduate university degree from Harvard (or any other university), I consider myself to have a doctorate in the Entrepreneurial School of Tough Lessons—but it hasn't come without a major investment. When your company's accrued revenue of a million dollars vanishes within a few short weeks, there are significant lessons to be learned both personally and professionally. And when you combine those experiences with the formal training I signed up for after starting my business, it is clear to me that learning while on the job provides a life-and-death element that no academic program can equal.

It has taken years for my confidence and self-esteem to expand in relation to the success of my business, but I have arrived and modestly feel that my cup runneth over with exuberance and enthusiasm to tackle any challenge thrown at my company and me. But let's go back to the beginning.

When I got my first office job, I had no idea what my super-powers were. The first thing I did on my lunch break was buy myself a briefcase—which today I find adorable and hilarious. Then, I went to a bookstore and bought myself a business magazine with a section on leadership. I knew nothing about business and leadership, but I figured that if I had a few buzzwords to throw around, no one would notice this girl had no idea what she was talking about.

It was clear, even to myself at the time, I was a clever, inde-pendent survivor who never looked back. Later on, I applied for a position with a recruiting firm, and confidence car-ried the day. Within a year, I was one of the company's top producers, and they began sending me to training and net-working opportunities throughout North America. I grew into a blossoming professional.

It was because of moments like these, which continue to this day, that I never minded the fact that I didn't have a degree. I have also since learned that the average entrepreneur, and some of the most successful in the world, didn't have col-lege degrees when they started out either. Isn't it funny, in a way, that these luminaries have been recognized by some of the most prestigious academic institutions in the world, receiving honorary PhDs for their achievements?

While I didn't mind not having a PhD (not even an honorary one), I *did* mind the fact that many Creative Niche clients and candidates didn't know I owned the company—they were under the impression the president owned it! They were not at fault. It wasn't like I did anything to advertise who I was and what my role was within the company. My title was director. I worked, went home to my family, and was otherwise pretty shy. I rarely networked, especially with my fellow entrepreneurs. That had to change.

Coming out of the Great Recession, I was only thirty-two years old, highly engaged in my business as I loved working, and had a lot of life left in me. I realized that if I was going to elevate my company to the next level, I had to advance *myself* to the next level first.

It was time to invest in myself!

STRATEGIC COACH

My first outside professional development investment was with Strategic Coach, a company that provides entrepreneurs with tools and time systems so they can focus on scaling and growing their business while also having balance.

At the time, I was hard-pressed to qualify for the course, not to mention pay for the tuition, which was significant. However, I reasoned it was now or never—time to grow some wings so I could fly!

As I think about it now, I was like a pilgrim who had been marching in the hot sun for a month with little water and food. After being rescued and sitting at a full table, all I could do was stuff as much liquid and food into my body as possible. The only difference was that I was cramming the information from the program into my spirit and mind.

THE ENTREPRENEURS' ORGANIZATION (EO)

My learning didn't stop with Strategic Coach. Next, I joined the Entrepreneurs' Organization (EO), where, for the first time, I had the chance to actually speak and relate to my fellow entrepreneurs.

Before EO, I was pretty reclusive. I was so caught up in work and family that I didn't know a group like this actually existed—and once I did, I was incredibly nervous about joining. It didn't matter that I'd been a reasonably successful entrepreneur for several years. I still had a case of imposter syndrome. I began telling myself that I was neither good enough nor smart enough to be there. Has that ever happened to you? If so, you know how debilitating it can be.

Eventually, I got over my nerves, accepted the fact that my fears were only in my head, enrolled in the program, and set out to enjoy myself while building new relationships.

At my first meeting, we sat at a round table, and everyone introduced themselves and their business. Then we followed the EO forum format: each person gave a five- to- seven-minute update on the progress of their business. It wasn't about giving or receiving advice, but more about sharing experiences and outcomes.

I'd been a little skeptical about the process at first, but once I saw it in action—and realized that I had gone through everything the other members were talking about—I was hooked.

I loved having a network full of new people in my life, my de facto board of advisors, that I could go to with any business or personal problem. After every meeting, I always walked away feeling like I had a new game plan, new strengths, and new knowledge. Whether I was flying high on an idea or having a breakdown about a situation, they always provided me with new insight, inspiration, and solutions to explore.

What I appreciated so much about EO was the sense of shared experience. They, too, had hired, grown, and scaled. They, too, had top-line financial milestones and goals they had to work towards.

They, too, had been forced to let people go or had lost staff who were invaluable to their business. They, too, had endured sleepless nights worrying about their business. They, too, had experienced the highest of highs and the lowest of lows.

Before I joined EO, I rode those highs and lows and everything in between like the Lone Ranger, and it wasn't healthy. As an entrepreneur, you don't want to freak anybody out, whether it's your employees or your partner at home. Even if the communication lines are wide open at home, it's not fair to your spouse or family to unload your burdens every day. If nothing else, you don't want them to worry about something without it being properly explained. Being married to an entrepreneur is not a walk in the park, so recognize your spouse for being there to mentally, emotionally, and physically sustain you.

At EO, I could finally explain my challenges to those other than my staff and family, to professionals who understood where I was coming from and who had no agenda or judgment with regards to what we were discussing. They had endured the same highs and lows, as well as identified important strategies and tactics for managing both the business and the personal sides of entrepreneurship. Finally, I was with people who understood the lifestyle, the pressure, and the fun that came with it.

I've had great friends in my life, but in EO, I felt like I'd found my tribe. The friends I made there are lifetime friends. It's easy to create deep bonds when you have so much in common, and you're all living the same lifestyle. Thanks to the way EO was set up, we arrived at an honest and raw place with each other very quickly. Especially as a Canadian who tends to get caught up in social pleasantries, it was refreshing to get down to brass tacks.

THE EO/MIT ENTREPRENEURIAL MASTER'S PROGRAM (EMP)

After building my confidence, I applied to the EO/MIT Entrepreneurial Master's Program (EMP). In my application letter, I shared my story, why I enjoyed being an entrepreneur, and what I wanted to do with my business in the future. I also wrote about my upbringing, my challenges, my desire to grow, and why I would be honored to be accepted into the program.

EMP is a three-year program with a student body of sixty-eight global entrepreneurs. Every year, students are required to attend four, fourteen-hour days. It's hard work, full of lessons from specialists, team-based business case studies, networking, and literally anything else that could be packed into that time frame.

The course provided a global perspective of business, relating the conversation all the way to where business begins:

in our respective communities. It was hard work, but it was equally rewarding and extremely inspirational. It was thanks to this program I decided to open new offices in Amsterdam and Cincinnati. I couldn't help it. One of the program presenters talked about taking your business global, and he hooked my imagination and interest from the outset. We'll get into the details of that story in the next chapter. For now, I'll just say it didn't go as planned.

YOUNG PRESIDENTS' ORGANIZATION (YPO)

These days, I'm primarily involved with the Young Presidents' Organization (YPO), which is similar to EO in many ways, but they have a higher threshold for inclusion. YPO is focused on attracting more experienced business leaders—which, in addition to entrepreneurs, also includes presidents and CEOs of corporations. In addition to the revenue criteria, YPO also has standards for inclusionary criteria such as top-line revenue, number of employees, payroll costs, and other related items.

At YPO, you meet two different types of people:

1. Entrepreneurs like me who oftentimes put themselves last but wish they had invested in themselves years ago.
2. Entrepreneurial executives who are on top of everything, see the value of investing in themselves, and get involved right out of the gate.

It's a mixed bag, but just as in EO, I've never met anyone who regretted joining—definitely not me.

One point that has been driven home during my time at YPO is: what you get out of an experience is proportionate to what you put into it. If you want to get value out of being part of an organization, then you have to put some thought and energy into it. You need to make it to the meetings and be present. It's easy to say you're a part of an organization, but in order to truly benefit, you have to be fully invested.

That's why I'm so proud to sit on the board of an incredible community of leaders and entrepreneurs at YPO. Every day, there is value and insight to be had, and I get to be surrounded by some of the most successful and coolest people I've ever met. Everywhere you turn, there are people who want nothing more than to help you, to talk with you, and to share their experiences. It's all about learning from each other, whether personally or professionally. Wouldn't it be fantastic if the world was a little more like that?

THE BELL LEADERSHIP INSTITUTE

Dr. Bell was introduced to me through the EO/MIT EMP and became perhaps the most influential mentor in my professional development. So much so that I have provided a detailed description of my experiential development with the institute in chapter 8.

THE BEST INVESTMENT YOU CAN MAKE

As entrepreneurs, we are always talking about investing in a new website, investing in new staff, investing in new ideas, but we don't look at an investment in ourselves like education and inspirational opportunities. And that, my friends, is a huge disconnect. Don't fall into that trap.

The earlier you can build up and reinforce your ability as a leader, the more fun you can have with it, and the more satisfying it will be. But think of how much more enriching it will be for your employees to have a leader they can trust and who is ready to invest in them. That's how you build a solid foundation for your business that will be sustainable for many years to come.

After years of riding out the effects of the recession, we were ready to grow again. I had learned a lot in the past few years, but one of the most important lessons was that sometimes giving your all to the business means giving your all to yourself. I thought success would be derived from giving my business everything I had, but because I hadn't been developing myself, everything I had wasn't good enough.

I realized that investing in my own professional development would provide innumerable benefits to my business, and amazing things would happen. The company wins if I'm better, and that realization has transformed my trajectory as a young entrepreneur.

Before investing in Strategic Coach, EO, EMP, and YPO, I thought that investing only had to do with things like office space and technology. When I finally learned to invest in myself as well, I found a treasure trove of helpful resources, knowledge, and support I didn't even know had existed. Sure, there would still be stressful days ahead, but from now on, I wouldn't have to go it alone. There were other entrepreneurs out there who could help me, and I was no longer afraid to open myself and let them share their expertise with me, as I do for them.

I knew I belonged, and with my newfound confidence, I was ready to take on the world. In essence, that is why I chose to write this book: to share my experience and lessons learned with you, as others have shared with me. Pass it on, and more will come back to you.

CHAPTER 7

THE IDEA MACHINE IS OUT OF CONTROL

CHAOS APPEARS WHEN YOU LEAST EXPECT IT

As I reflect on my entrepreneurial career, I realize that a major contribution to my success has been my decisiveness. You could even call it one of my signature moves or unique abilities.

For instance, when it came time to open a new office in Ottawa (see chapter 3), I didn't hesitate. I'd known the team member who facilitated that opening for years. She was and still is a rock star. I believed in her 100 percent. Six weeks later, the office was open and quickly became a huge contributing component of the organization. Opening the Ottawa office was one of the best business decisions I'd ever made up until that time.

However, my decisiveness has also bitten me on the behind on more than a couple of occasions. For example, in 2011, fresh off my experience at EMP, I decided to take Creative Niche International and establish offices in Amsterdam and Cincinnati. After all, an office in the United States felt like a no-brainer. And I was already generating business with a French-based company too, so why not open an office in Europe to provide better customer service?

Within six months and a considerable investment of time and money, my dream had come true: we were truly an international company, with offices in three different countries. I'd love to say that those offices would mark the first of many or that those offices were still alive and well. Alas, neither statement would be true.

Going global didn't work out for a variety of reasons:

- I took too much on by trying to open two locations at once.
- I didn't make the right choices in selecting staff.
- The promised business development in Europe never materialized.
- We weren't aware of cultural differences in Europe, especially with regard to employment law.

I'd been so excited by the potential to expand, but in hindsight, it was clear that my eagerness to open those offices had given us little chance to succeed. There was too much I didn't know or had failed to account for, and instead of taking the time to address these unknowns, I focused only on the upside, willing our offices to succeed rather than following a strategic plan to make it so.

I had my reasons for not thinking clearly about Amsterdam and Cincinnati. In truth, my attention was divided. On or about the same time we were expanding, I received an unexpected and unwelcome surprise.

My primary business development agent at the time was my sister and best friend, Jenny. One day, she came to me and said, "You know that bump I showed you when we were away a few weeks ago? They said it was a fibroid tumour. I'm sure it's nothing, but would you mind coming with me for my follow-up consultation?"

Strong-minded as she was, I knew she was making every effort to put on a brave face, and with just cause. Our mother had fibroid tumours when she was younger, and so had Jenny. Her doctors said they weren't worried, but they wanted to do a biopsy as a precaution.

Something about that conversation didn't feel right. I felt a knot tighten in my gut, and it started to grow as we left for home.

Her follow-up appointment was at eleven o'clock the next

day. When I picked her up, I could tell she hadn't slept a wink due to her anxiety. Still, I wanted to get her in a positive mindset, so we went out for breakfast, shopped at a boutique, and then headed off to the hospital.

Neither of us was prepared for what came next. In the movies, doctors talk to you in a closed office. They sit you down at their desk, open an important-looking folder, and break the bad news as gently as possible.

Not in real life.

My sister and I waited for the doctor in a small hospital room, where the only divider between us and the others in the room was a set of sliding curtains. The doctor came in, and before closing the curtains, he said, "I have bad news. You have cancer."

His words were devastating. My sister was a single mom with two young daughters, and a cancer diagnosis would be incredibly difficult for her to manage alone. To add insult to injury, the more we learned, the more we realized how serious her condition was. The tumour was already quite large, and it had spread to her lymph nodes. The doctors recommended that she begin chemotherapy right away. And thus began our journey on the cancer carousel, as we attended every appointment together.

I don't want to sound like a soap opera, but things were

also risky at Creative Niche; the timing couldn't have been worse. I was frustrated with the two offices that I'd staked a lot of hope and capital on; my sister, best friend, and top salesperson would be out of the office for several months; the company culture was slipping into the toilet; and my relationship with the president had become more strained, to say the least.

By this point, he'd become passive-aggressive, muttering comments about me when I was within earshot. The staff soaked it up. They still felt burned from the failing expansion experiment, which had taken considerable focus and resources from the core business.

To top things off, between my sister and work and being a mom to two young boys, my marriage suffered.

The result of everything had taken its toll. I had fallen out of love with my company and didn't know how to reignite the spark.

SISTER TIME

Jenny's illness, treatment, and recovery process would take a year from start to finish. The first six months were the most intense.

Frankly, I wasn't handling it very well.

All I could think about was what life would be like without my sister. I couldn't help it. I knew it was just the fear talking, but since she had such a huge presence in my life and my business, I began to doubt everything.

All I wanted to do was escape: to quit work, quit cancer, and find some peace and tranquillity.

Despite my utter lack of motivation, I knew I had to buckle down and get shit done and face the music.

Most importantly, I would never leave my sister's side when she needed me the most.

Early in the process of Jenny's treatment, I printed out a picture of the Eiffel Tower, put it in a frame, and placed it in her living room, where she would see it every day. She loved France and had even lived there for a year. I promised her we'd travel there when she finished her chemo, and so we did.

During the summer, we hopped on a plane and flew to Amsterdam—with a visit to Paris. The night before my sister and I said *au revoir*, I had an epiphany while lying awake in bed: "Close the Amsterdam and Cincinnati offices." I'd felt burned by the failure of our offices—and why not? "Successful entrepreneurs" don't like to fail at anything, and I was no different. But that night, I was finally able to push my feelings aside and accept the fact that the only way to move forward was without those offices. The global experiment had seemed like a good idea, but it was over.

The next morning, I told my finance manager, "I need you to analyze Amsterdam and Cincinnati. Let's wrap up our books. I'm going to put a plan in place to let our staff go and service the business from Canada. I'll fly to Amsterdam to make that happen, and it will all be behind us. I want it completely shut down in three weeks." I didn't try to spin the narrative at all. I had decided to close the offices, and that was the end of it.

After arriving in Amsterdam, I formally began the process of unwinding the business. When I finished doing what I needed to do, we hopped on a train to Paris and had an incredible time together, including a well-earned visit to the Eiffel Tower.

The past several months had been rough, but I didn't harbour any regrets. The global experiment hadn't worked, but it still led to a vast array of benefits to our company in the long run. For one, we'd opened the doors to tier-one entrepreneurs in both Europe and the United States in a major way. Further, the business lessons we learned during that time were amazing. It didn't work out, but I was ready to get more learning under my belt.

In fact, after the Paris trip, my creative juices were beginning to stir again. Hope sprang eternal. My sister was recuperating nicely, and I was finally able to be honest with myself about the mistake I had made in opening our two expansion offices.

Slowly but surely, my life began to simplify. No more excessive travel, no more servicing markets we didn't understand, and no more freaking cancer. I felt like a million bucks. Now, all I had to do was find a way to fall back in love with my business.

GETTING OUT OF THE BUBBLE

The Amsterdam and Cincinnati offices were symptomatic of what I consider my high-growth years. I was learning so much; I wanted to put these thoughts into action, and I wanted to share all my great ideas.

At least, I thought my ideas were great, and I thought my employees did as well. Every time I shared a new idea with them, they looked enthusiastic and seemed genuinely interested (even if, as I learned later, they were screaming on the inside). I assumed that if they didn't like my ideas, they would tell me, but that wasn't the case.

They certainly had plenty of opportunities to do so because I was throwing ideas at them left and right. Being an idea machine is part of the entrepreneur's job description. It's what we do for survival. If we don't think of new ideas and ways to improve our operations, then our companies won't evolve, and if that doesn't happen, we won't be sustainable. It's essential that we constantly be on the lookout for new products, methodologies, and enhanced technologies, as well as redesigning our corporate structures and business models.

But it's also important to know which ideas are winners and which are duds. Otherwise, an entrepreneur's greatest gift—being an idea machine—can also become their greatest weakness.

During most of this period, I had no way of distinguishing between the winners and losers because no one felt empowered enough to tell me. I'd walk into a meeting and hijack the agenda. "You know what?" I'd say, "That reminds me of a book I read this weekend that had a neat case study about something another company is doing. What do you guys think about that?"

Instead of gently pushing back or reminding me of the meeting's actual agenda, everyone at the meeting would nod their head, and then we'd start talking about this new possibility. Just like that, the meeting was hijacked, I'd wasted everyone's time, and I may have sent one or two employees on a needless hunt to research and implement the idea.

Situations like these are why some people think entrepreneurs exercise their power and take advantage of others. To be fair, they probably do, but in my case at least, it wasn't on purpose. I was energized by everything I was learning at the time and derived a lot of satisfaction from sharing my ideas. It was like a hit of dopamine.

The problem with my process was that these ideas were underdeveloped. They weren't being filtered properly, and I wasn't really seeking meaningful feedback. They were just a lazy dumping of ideas—and they were costing my business money and me a loss of credibility.

THE COST OF A GOOD (OR NOT SO GOOD) IDEA

When you're not the person doing the implementation, it's easy to forget that every new project you assign to an employee has a tremendous impact on their workload. Coming up with the idea is the easy part; the actual work is in making it operational.

My ideas were coming too rapidly for anyone to take any meaningful action on them. I would get an idea, then I would assign one or two people to look into it, as in: What did it mean for our business? What was the opportunity? How could we market it? How would we actually execute and operationalize it? How could we measure its success?

Every time I blurted out an idea, I took an employee off

course. Then, before they could come back to me with feedback, I had dumped another two more ideas on them. My staff were drowning in a sea of ideas—and most of them weren't any good!

This exercise of chasing wild geese began to take its toll. I may have been all-in on throwing out as many ideas as I could, but all I had to show for it was a team of distracted employees. Some were angry with my constant requests, some were frazzled from the effort they put in, and some had simply checked out, knowing all too well that I wasn't going to follow-up on half the projects I had assigned to them.

The personnel cost of realizing my ideas was the depletion of my employees' energy and desire for their jobs. What could be more detrimental to a business than to have an unmotivated workforce? It creates inefficiency, which ultimately causes a drop-off in profitability.

In retrospect, my staff weren't focused on their job positions anymore; they were paying attention to work activity that wasn't generating any revenue and often never would. My "ideas" were not part of a strategic plan. They were just distractions I had created and dumped on my staff and then walked away. By the time I understood the impact of these diversions, the damage had already been done.

If you're not soliciting feedback from your team on an ongoing basis—especially on ideas that may affect the operation of your company—you may not be the leader you would like to be. I know that is how I felt, and I knew something had to change.

THE LEADERSHIP TEAM

A good leader determines when an idea is worth pursuing by doing a preliminary risk/benefit assessment. If it passes subsequent appraisal, and the benefit is worth the human resource investment, they can submit it to staff for two-way feedback, especially those who will be impacted by it the most.

In that regard, I wasn't doing my job as a leader. Luckily, I soon had the privilege of learning exactly how my employees felt about my idea dumps. They rightly believed that I regularly dropped the ball by assigning a task to someone to work with me on it, and then I would do nothing.

My employees were frustrated with me for overcomplicating their lives with ideas that never went anywhere. None of this was intentional, of course, but it was the reality all the same.

To address this problem, the first step I took was to develop a leadership team composed of five respected staff from different departments of the company. In addition, I wanted to limit the amount of time that was invested in introducing new ideas, so I resolved not to meet more than once per month.

When we met, I would present an idea, explain how it came to fruition, and then make a case for what it could do for our business. Then, I opened the door for honest feedback. Some people would say, "It's not a bad idea. But we're pretty focused on this other project right now, so let's keep it on ice." And some others would say, "This is so far outside of what we do, I don't see us being able to pull it off. Financially it's a huge investment." If there was interest in pursuing something, we deferred detailed discussion until the next meeting, with one or two people doing some secondary analysis to be presented at that time.

Whatever their response, I needed to hear it. No matter what, I was going to be an idea machine again; that's just what entrepreneurs do. I imagined I would continue to bolt upright in the middle of the night with some random possibility buzzing in my brain that super excited me. But with my leadership team, I had a group of people who would help me create discipline, structure, and rigour around these ideas. No more drive-by delegation or half-assed briefs.

From now on, I would only share my ideas in a specific way and in the appropriate context so that my team understood the value proposition the idea might have and what needed to happen internally for us to be successful with it. I also invited them to present new concepts at our meetings and suggested they would be high-value since they had the experience of being on the front lines.

FINDING BALANCE

I still believe in being an idea machine and striking on good ideas when the iron is hot. An entrepreneur who isn't constantly looking to improve outputs isn't fully committed. The missed opportunities and inaction that arise from maintaining the status quo can be even more damaging to your business than overcommitting. When you stop taking risks, your business begins to slowly die.

I've certainly learned the value of making informed decisions and not chasing every idea that crosses my mind down the proverbial rabbit hole. These days, aside from the invaluable help of my leadership team, I have a process for identifying good ideas—and it's a lot more than just blurting them out and seeing what happens. With every idea, there are three questions I ask myself, courtesy of a Creative Niche team member:

1. Will it make us better?
   A. More profitable?
   B. More attractive to active/prospective clients?
   C. Reduced turnover with staff?
2. How will we know if it's successful?

D. Desired outcomes?
3. What direct investment, training, or headcount do we need to develop and test this idea?

If, after answering these questions, the idea still sounds worthwhile, then I take it to my leadership team. And since the idea has been given a little extra consideration, I'm able to provide the team with enough context to enable them to provide me with more relevant feedback and suggestions. Then, together with their input, we have the necessary perspective to proceed to the next step in the decision-making process by completing a detailed cost-benefit analysis.

It doesn't matter who you run your ideas past. It could be your own personal advisory board, a fellow entrepreneur, or other thought leaders. You may even want to talk it out with a larger company executive who may have tried something similar, or perhaps a finance or consulting company to help you run the numbers. Whoever you talk to, your goal is the same: to lay it all out and make the decision easy, one way or the other. Trust me: it's better to prove an idea wrong than to implement a flawed concept.

Like me, you may have times when a "great idea" is passed on to you, but because of other projects or your business's overall strategic vision, you'll have to delay its implementation. It might be a painful "no" at the moment, but it will keep your business moving forward far more effectively.

Besides, since the idea has been shared and documented, when the timing is right, you can reintroduce it, and if approved, it will be easier to implement than it would have been if you hadn't waited.

DON'T FORGET TO ENGAGE YOUR TEAM

When it was just my staff of four and me, it was easy to make a decision on my own and say, "Let's do it." My business was very small, and I knew I could get my employees on board fairly quickly.

But even then, it was a tough sell. Sure, I had a plan for how I wanted everything to get done, but I didn't invite anyone into the decision-making process. I didn't invite them to share the excitement or be part of the work. I just decided to move us into a larger office one day, or open an entirely new office in Amsterdam.

Entrepreneurs are great salespeople. We sell our products to clients and our vision to employees, and we can be extremely persuasive about it. We'll come at you with a big presentation, improvise if needed, and we'll bullshit with the best of them. We can sell anything under the sun—except buy-in. That only comes through engagement.

It took me a year and several hundred thousand dollars to learn this lesson.

It wasn't that I was trying to be manipulative or on a power trip; I just naively thought that everyone would think my idea was great because *I* thought it was great. I thought they would be excited because *I* was excited. But because I didn't engage them, and because I didn't invite them into the process, they were left feeling bewildered and confused. If you don't give them a stake in your decision-making process, then all you're doing is creating another distraction.

You're just adding work that will eventually overwhelm and alienate valuable team members, which, in turn, will increase your turnover rates. And, as you know, that will cost you money.

Instead, give your team a stake in the decision-making process. Identify the team members whose work your decision impacts the most, and involve them in the process. These team members can help you understand what additional resources you may need, what a realistic time frame is for execution, and how to plan out your idea in a way that doesn't harm your business. By so doing, you will have a better understanding of the variables involved before making a costly mistake.

At the end of the day, you're still the one who makes the decisions, and you're still the one who has to see it through. Until you execute, you'll never know for sure whether your idea works. And if the idea *doesn't* work, you will want to have your team stand with you. Otherwise, it's not just your idea that's in trouble, but your culture as well.

CHAPTER 8

RESETTING THE CULTURE

WHEN IN DOUBT, LOOK IN THE MIRROR

When your company culture is falling apart, and you are hanging on by a thread, I have learned the best place to look when you aren't sure what's causing the problem is *in the mirror*!

My wake-up call began through my participation in an off-shoot course from my MIT/EMP experience. During my second year, an older gentleman, Dr. Bell, was the leader for much of the content on our second day. He was an amazing human, a fantastic teacher, and a renowned leadership coach. Working out of his institute in Chapel Hill, North Carolina, he had provided leadership training to professional athletes, politicians, entrepreneurs, and Fortune 500 executives to facilitate their growth and development. Likewise, he not only provided content but also direct mentoring and consultation to clients who managed some of the biggest mergers and acquisitions in history.

His presence, leadership, and approach to teaching absolutely fascinated me. The positive, role model leaders he described resonated to the core of my being. They were the exact kind of leaders I wanted to be. His message inspired me to grow up and embrace his unique perspective on leadership.

So when I learned I could register for his executive leadership program at his institute in Chapel Hill, North Carolina, I did—and by the end of that day, I had already booked my flight!

As a prerequisite to the program, participants must provide the names of various people in their lives, both personally and professionally, including ex-employees, direct and indirect employees, romantic partners, friends, vendors, you name it. I provided a spreadsheet of all their names, email addresses, and phone numbers, and then I forgot all about it.

After arriving at the institute a few months afterwards, I met roughly twenty other participants, but they weren't really like me. They were mostly older men, the majority of which were CEOs of major corporations.

The program was made up of a series of lectures. On the first day, the lecture outlined the guiding principles of leadership focused on what leaders should think about, such as how team members may want to be treated. We covered the principles of developing and leading teams from a very basic level. I soaked it up, filling pages and pages of notes.

On day two, I felt more comfortable in the lecture room and was fairly relaxed as the assistants handed out binders to everyone. A quiet came over the room as Dr. Bell entered and said, "We're going to break early today. We asked the people in your lives to complete a survey using our proprietary leadership platform. Remember that list you filled out before coming? We have provided you with the results of the survey for you to better understand your leadership style. Behind tab five, you will find the positive feedback you received, and behind tab six, the negative feedback. I recommend you go find a bench somewhere, maybe go for a walk first, and then read the positive comments. After you have finished, you can read the negative page, but when you've done with that, go back and review the positive feedback again. Do some serious thinking and reflect on what you are about to learn. I'll see you in the morning."

Very few participants followed his instructions. CEOs are a competitive sort, after all. I watched as almost everybody in the room grabbed their binders, skipped right past the positive feedback on tab five, and went straight to tab six.

Everyone wanted to read the negative things, and why not? If there weren't any bad comments, you would be a good leader and could relax.

Well, when in Rome, I thought as I opened my binder to the negative comments like everyone else.

I didn't know exactly what to expect from my binder. I liked Dr. Bell and his program, and I saw great value in the exercise and what it stood for, but would it really benefit me? While I suspected I had my flaws, I also knew I was relatively well-liked, to the point I thought I would score pretty high on my leadership assessment—maybe a seven out of ten.

When I opened my binder, I was dumbfounded. Staring back at me was a list of words that you would never want to see describing yourself: control freak, has trust issues, over-commits, under delivers, starts projects she doesn't finish, late for meetings, doesn't show up for meetings, inconsiderate of other people's time, disorganized, plays favourites, is unfair, and is passive-aggressive.

I flipped back to the cover to make sure I'd received the right binder. Yep, it was mine.

My heart started to pound furiously, my face turned bright red, and I felt as though I was going to burst into tears. For a while, I just sat there numb, and then I started to feel sorry for myself. It was all I could do to keep from exploding.

Then the anger set in, "How could they possibly understand what it was like to be me? They didn't understand the stress of having everything on the line, the demands and pressure I had day after day. They didn't know I was going home and working every night, putting my personal life on the line to keep my business running. They didn't have to worry about the fact that taking a day off meant the company might not meet its financial commitments or how our reputation could suffer. They didn't know what it was like to lose nearly a million dollars that almost cost me my business. They didn't appreciate *me* or everything I did for the business.

I sat with my anger a little longer and then let it go. Of course, they didn't know these things. I never told them. I never shared anything!

All this time, I thought I was protecting my team. But I wasn't. All I was doing was hurting them, hurting our relationship, and their connection to the business. Even worse, I was negatively impacting my own emotional well-being and mental health.

Clarity prevailed, and gratitude overwhelmed me. I could only imagine the courage it took to give this kind of feedback to me—but the fact they did it meant they cared! In that regard, it was good to know my staff liked me, but I realized it was better to be respected than to be liked.

After my look in the mirror, I concluded that I had some serious work to do in order to better understand why these behaviours were showing up in my professional life. In that moment, I saw the light, and I promised myself I would start the journey toward becoming the leader my staff deserved.

WHAT DO YOU DO WHEN YOU'RE THE PROBLEM?

I wanted to express my gratitude to my staff for what they had said about me—more importantly, I wanted to communicate what I was going to do about each bit of feedback I'd received. So, on my flight home, I created a slide deck. The first slide had all the positive feedback comments, with direct quotes from the binder to give them context. The second slide did the same with all the negative responses.

When I returned to work, I called a company staff meeting. Looking around the room, I could see that many people were nervous. In fact, it was easy to tell who had participated in the survey—they were the ones who appeared as though they were going to get sick, pass out, or both!

I brought up the slide deck. I explained that I had participated in this leadership course and why I had done so. Then, I began, "When I walked into the course lecture room for the first time, I thought I was a good leader. But when I left for home, I realized I had a lot of work to do before becoming the leader you guys deserve." I thanked the team for its feedback and for helping me to become a better person.

Then, I shared that feedback.

After a few good laughs at my expense, I opened up to them. I admitted I had trouble welcoming feedback because I felt dumb or inadequate. Other times, I had trouble with it because I didn't want to acknowledge when I was struggling, nor did I want them to carry my worries and fears.

Then I told them I didn't want to be that person anymore. I didn't want those words to describe my leadership style. I wanted to earn their trust and respect. I was determined to do the work to convert their feedback into actionable tasks so I could aspire to become a better leader.

I could actually feel the tension in the room lift and float out the door as the meeting continued. I had addressed the elephant in the room, and it was immediately noticeable and a major step in the change process of our culture. In order for our company culture to advance and move forward, the process had to start with me. So I owned up to who I was—and admitted to the fact that I had not been my best self.

Of course, this meeting didn't repair the damage over-night. Words are words, and I still had to follow through on my promises. I needed to stop bombing people with ideas and start setting realistic expectations for every-one, myself included. I learned from this exercise and follow-up communications that giving and receiving feed-back is a key element in becoming a well-rounded person and entrepreneur. I am so grateful for realizing this truth at such a crucial time of evolution for both my company and me.

None of these things were core strengths for me, so I con-tracted with a business coach to help me become more accountable and strengthen weak muscles.

COACHING UP

I was unsure about hiring a coach, as some of my friends had worked with business coaches before, and they had mixed feedback about the experiences. Some of them thought working with a coach was a waste of time and money, while others found their coach contributed to them growing their business by 20 percent or more.

I understand why some people might have a negative experi-ence with a coach. If you don't connect with the person, or if you're not ready to be honest, transparent, and vulnerable—in other words, if you're not ready to do the work—then it's probably not going to work out well for you. But in my case, I was definitely prepared to move forward.

Since I didn't want to lose control of my business and financial stability, mitigate my leadership effectiveness, or witness our company culture disintegrate before my very eyes, I *was* willing to listen, learn, and have a great experience with my business coach.

When we started working together, I was very honest about my history. I shared what I had learned about myself in leadership training, what I learned about business at EMP, where I thought the business was today, and what we needed to do to move forward. Quickly, she identified several issues—most of which I'd already known but didn't have the courage to tackle head-on. As an entrepreneur, I was a warrior in many ways, but up to that point, confrontation hadn't been one of my strong suits.

This weakness, however, was the root of our culture problem. I was the entrepreneur, I led by example, I set the tone for business development. But if I wasn't stepping up and holding people accountable for their behaviour, then I was giving everyone a free pass, which wasn't fair to them, and definitely not advantageous for the company.

My coach let me know all of this in no uncertain terms and that it was time to develop a plan of action to change it.

I admit it was scary, especially because it meant reducing or changing staff and how I could do that? I hired them, trained them, and now I might be firing them? Wasn't I at fault for this outcome? My head started to spin...

Luckily, my coach brought me back to reality. We focused our conversations on two things: the employee's ability to produce and their ability to contribute positively to the culture. For each employee I had to:

- Identify strengths and weaknesses.
- Determine if they were trainable for success or just a bad fit.
- Ascertain competency, compatibility with the business, and their motivation.
- Identify if they were problematic on the culture side.

After establishing the prescriptive criteria, we identified the first step in the assessment process and my desired outcome.

We also determined the timelines, and finally, after numerous role-play sessions, my coach helped me to access the skills I needed to participate in those conversations effectively and humanely.

This process was invaluable to me, as I'm not always the best communicator. I can be alternatively too strong or too passive. I was very worried about how my feedback would impact my colleagues, whether I would hurt someone's feelings, and, if I did, how it would further affect the culture. On the other hand, I fully understood the importance and benefit of developing my feedback muscle in professional and personal relationships. So, I threw myself into the prep work, and soon enough, it was time to execute.

At first, the interviews were awkward and horrible, but very necessary. I walked into every meeting with sweaty palms and a shaky voice, but that didn't stop me from delivering important feedback and laying down measurable expectations. I followed up every meeting with an email about what we had discussed and what we all needed to do to move forward together. Just as I had been coached and practised, I was always specific about my expectations and the timeline.

Some great people resigned during this period, along with some not-so-greats. Our talks helped them realize the same thing I had known: for whatever reason, those team members were no longer their best selves at the company. Maybe they were a bit bored, maybe they couldn't get over the mistakes they'd made in the past, or maybe they couldn't get over the many challenges the company had faced.

Whatever the reason, I didn't blame them for their feelings. In fact, in many ways, I felt responsible for them—and I admitted as much to them. It can be hard to look at things with a fresh perspective when you've already been through so much shit to get there. Between the recession, my sister's illness, and my own spotty record as a leader, working at Creative Niche hadn't been all wine and roses for staff.

Others chose to stay—and afterwards, they were incredible, and I was happy to have them. Prior to these interviews, determining whether a team member would choose to resign or stay on board wasn't the big goal.

It was to hold people to account and to reset the culture. If they wanted to go, now was the time. If they wanted to stay, that was great too—as long as they committed to the timelines and expectations we had laid out for them, which they all did.

By confronting the issues plaguing the company, we'd hit a hard reset on our culture and had given Creative Niche a second chance.

Slowly, I began to fall back in love with my business.

STYLE AND FIT

Most, if not all, companies need a culture reset from time to time to keep pace with the change in technologies, work ethic values, and target markets. It's part of the growth process and ensures there is good style and fit within your corporate structure. In an effective organization, everyone can't be a leader, and without an effective team, nothing would get done. When hiring, it is important to consider the behaviours of your current team relative to those you may be bringing on board, as well as new hires' enthusiasm for and acceptance of the company culture and values. If compatibility and effectiveness are in place, then you have a positive corporate style and fit and stronger potential for achieving success.

But even in the best environments, even when you're able to create the best outcomes, sometimes you will have to fire people. That, too, is part of the territory.

I have had to personally let more than fifteen people go during my time at Creative Niche—which, all things considered, is a good turnover ratio for companies in our sector. The reasons for each dismissal vary, but often you'll know in your gut from the outset of the interview that there's a problem. Maybe the team member isn't a good culture fit, maybe they're not performing up to their ability, maybe they're not committed, or maybe they're just unpleasant to be around.

Chances are, you already know who you'd rather not keep on your team. If you're not sure, here's a little exercise: Imagine you have to fire everyone in your company. Who would you rehire enthusiastically? Chances are, you wouldn't bring everyone back.

For those you wouldn't bring back, the question is simple: can they be coached up, or is it not worth the trouble?

As soon as you know a team member isn't a good fit, don't hesitate to fire them. I know this might sound cold—and I also know many entrepreneurs do everything they can to put this off—but trust me on this one. It doesn't matter how skilled they are. Keeping them around can badly damage your culture and cause you to lose people who *are* a good fit. The longer a problem employee stays around, the more the good employees will lose respect for you and lose faith in the business. I made the mistake of keeping problem employees around while my attention was elsewhere, and it almost cost me my entire company.

If you're still not convinced, look at it this way: keeping someone around who doesn't belong doesn't just hurt you and your company, it hurts that employee as well. Unhappy employees aren't stupid. They know if they're not successful, not getting along with the rest of the team and if things just aren't working out. The longer you keep them on the payroll, the longer they're stuck in limbo, unsure if they are coming or going. By letting them go, you're also giving them the chance to reset their career expectations and direction and hopefully find more happiness on the path they choose.

If you are going to let someone go, then it's important you

do it right. Here are some considerations to help you plan out the process.

WHAT IS THE FALLOUT?

When I fire someone, the first thing I think about is what kind of damage control I will need to put in place once the move has been made. No matter what, I know there will be some fallout, and I will need to be there to manage it, so I make sure I'm in town for at least a week afterwards.

Then, I identify who this firing is going to impact. Even toxic employees usually have at least one good relationship, and you will want to mitigate the damage with that person as best as you can. This is always my first priority.

Then, I broaden my scope to consider the overall culture. Unless it is after hours, I call a meeting as soon as I've walked that person out, so I can control the narrative and clear the air. Finally, to reaffirm my commitment to the team, I'll plan a social event of some sort with them, such as a lunch or a happy hour.

WHAT HAPPENS TO THEIR JOB?

When you let a person go, or when someone resigns, it's not a given that you're going to replace them. Maybe that role has become superfluous, or it's time to restructure responsibilities. If you lose someone from the headcount, consider taking half their salary and reallocate it to key staff and have them take on those responsibilities. It may be a great opportunity to improve efficiency and grow your employees and profit at the same time.

If you do intend to replace that team member, always look to internal options first. When someone leaves, it is an opportunity to promote or give a pay increase to someone who is an A-player.

KEEP THEIR FEELINGS IN MIND

It's okay if you're nervous letting someone go. I've done it a lot—and it's still uncomfortable!

I've tried to frame my approach with that team member's well-being in mind as much as possible. Part of that is to avoid dragging out the meeting. Letting someone go isn't a negotiation; it's a final decision. Be quick about it, and let them get on with their day.

I also avoid building any unnecessary suspense. Calendar invites are a no-go because they create a tremendous amount of anxiety. I also avoid having the meetings on Fridays, as I don't want the rest of the team spending the weekend fixated on what has happened, and I truly believe that letting someone go earlier in the week is better for the individual, allowing them time to process before the weekend comes around.

THE MEETING

At the meeting itself, you'll want to be prepared:

- Update yourself on and understand the applicable laws. If you aren't sure, engage an employment lawyer.
- Decide in advance the in lieu of work amount and severance you are offering (be generous).
- Have a witness, someone else besides you and the employee, in the room (or if virtually, on video).
- Do a couple of dry runs to help you once the nerves kick in.
- Have all the necessary paperwork organized and out on the table (or, if virtual, a draft with necessary attachments).
- Have class, be gracious, and thank them in a meaningful way for their contribution to your company.

My process is as follows: For the paperwork, specifically the termination letter and the release, I have it all ready and done well ahead of the meeting. Before the employee walks in, my witness is ready and waiting in the meeting room. Then, I approach the employee—let's call him Joe in this case—and ask him for five minutes.

When Joe walks in, I'll close the door and get down to business. "Joe, I've pulled you in here because, unfortunately, we're going to have to let you go. Now, what does that mean? It means that effective immediately, you are no longer an employee of Creative Niche."

Then, I stop talking and let that set in for a minute. I continue:

> "I know that's big news. I'm not sure if you're surprised by it, but I do want to give you some context. We've been having ongoing discussions about your ability to be successful here. One of the biggest commitments I made when I started this business was that I wanted everyone to feel like they were contributing to its success in a meaningful way.
>
> For whatever reason, we haven't realized that success together. I don't believe it's doing you or the company a service in keeping you on board. That's why I've made this serious decision. I haven't made it quickly. As you know full well, we've been having conversations for months now regarding your performance, and I was hoping that I would see the needle move, but it hasn't.
>
> We have some off-boarding documents I will go through with you; please feel free to ask any related questions. I also have a package here with your termination letter and your severance details. You can go over this when you leave.
>
> I know this may be overwhelming, and you're probably still processing everything right now. Let's go get your stuff from

your desk. We don't want it to be too disruptive or awkward, so we're going to ask that you exit the building. I know you have a great relationship with your colleagues, and you can reach out to them. We will be letting them know about your termination this afternoon. We're not going to say anything disparaging about you whatsoever. Why would we? You've been a great addition to the team, and we are going to miss you."

Then I move on to off-boarding. We locate their office keys, their computer and charger, and ask for all their passwords. We also have an official off-boarding document, which is very important for entrepreneurs. Then, we deactivate all their software platforms, so they no longer have access to anything. We walk them out, and then I immediately post a quick message on Slack to ask the team to gather in the big boardroom or virtually.

THE TEAM MEETING

When the team assembles, I say, "Hey, guys, the upside of having a familial culture is we become close and supportive of one another. The downside is when we have turnover. It's always difficult. We have a couple of staff announcements to make this morning. I want you to know we're not going through any type of restructuring. Everyone's job is safe. I want to give you some context as to why this happened."

When you let someone go, the rest of the team immediately

begins to wonder if they need to look for a new job. Junior staff members are especially sensitive to this.

They go to the worst-case scenario immediately. You have to tell them explicitly over and over, "We are not restructuring, and this is not a layoff situation. This has nothing to do with our financial performance."

But I do explain the context of the turnover. Afterwards, I immediately followed up with an all-staff message reiterating everything that I said.

WEATHERING RESIGNATIONS

When we let somebody go, we always wish them well and never speak ill of them. This isn't going to change how they feel about the situation, of course. No matter what your previous relationship, as soon as you let a person go, they don't like you—and understandably so. Being fired is traumatic, and it's natural for even the best people to feel victimized.

Entrepreneurs experience similar trauma when valued team members resign. There have certainly been occasions when a rock star team member said they were leaving, and I began to feel bitter or threatened about it. The following comments are representative of the feelings surrounding the departure of a key employee:

"Everyone likes them. How will the culture recover?"

"Are you kidding me? I've done so much to support them!"

"They had the strongest relationship with our key client. What happens if we lose them?"

"I have given them so much opportunity, and they have the audacity to resign right now when they know I need them the most?"

You're going to feel this way when people move on. It's only natural. Just remember that it's also natural for them to decide to advance their career to the next level. If you value them, then it's important that you not take their decision personally. Sure, you're going to have some bad feelings at first, and that's okay. Just get out of the office and go vent somewhere else, and then come back and celebrate them.

I get why entrepreneurs have trouble handling the blow of losing a valued team member. I don't like it either—but I always try to keep it classy. If you go around badmouthing that employee after they've resigned, you've created a poison pill for your culture. It may come from a protectionist impulse to try and rally the troops behind you, but it's likely to have the opposite effect.

So, when people resign from my company, I throw them

a party and buy them a gift. We celebrate them for their contributions, thank them for helping us grow, and relive our favourite memories with them. That way, even if they're no longer your employee, you can still enjoy a fruitful relationship with them.

Creative Niche always welcomes alumni back with open arms. Every year at the Christmas party, we often have one or two alumni who I haven't seen in a few years crash the party. It's great to catch up with them and learn about what they've been up to since they left.

TIME TO STAND FOR SOMETHING NEW

Looking back, I can attribute the success of this reset process to two things.

First was the class and consideration we showed our people at every step. I treated each team member with dignity, inviting them into a meaningful conversation about their career, what their next steps at Creative Niche would be, and what was expected of them in terms of the business and culture.

Second was my coach. This was a period of time of great growth for me, and I couldn't have done it without her. My coach taught me how to manage this transition with poise and professionalism. We worked on my leadership, management, communication, and expectation setting. For perhaps the first time, I was able to tell my people I knew what they needed to do, why they needed to do it, and the related timeline to completion. I became a better entrepreneur.

Now that we had effectively reset the culture, it was time to create a new identity, to reassert who we were, what we stood for, and what it was like to work for us.

CHAPTER 9

NEW VALUES, NEW IDENTITY

UNDER NEW MANAGEMENT

Now that we had effectively reset the culture, it was time to reinvent ourselves in the likeness of successful professionals, to assert our company values, and to exemplify a positive work environment based on mutual respect, honest communications, and thoughtful leadership.

I had lost a lot of cultural capital with my team, but I was determined to earn it back. As fate would have it, my president resigned right around this time. When chaos pays you a visit, you have to step back from the situation you are encountering and ask, "Is this a good thing or a bad thing?" In this case, I was grateful for his contribution to building the company, but I was ready to retake the helm and set sail for our next destination.

His resignation brought greater clarity to how the leadership structure at the company was perceived and defined. For some time, staff had been having difficulty understanding the difference between the president's role and my role, and that ambiguity wasn't going to contribute to our cultural rebuild.

Now that it was just me, I anticipated being able to bring clarity and purpose to our new mission: rebuild our culture and do it together! I wanted our culture to reflect positive values we would be proud of and our workspace to be a place where everyone looked forward to coming to every day.

Now that I was leading the company again, I wanted to show the team I was committed to their future success and to that of the company.

While I had never literally been away, it was important for me to know that they knew I was back and ready to rekindle relationships and collaborate in achieving our respective goals. Finally, it would be important to give and receive feedback on an ongoing basis in order to better understand the shortcomings in our business processes, identify individual strengths of team members, and figure out how we would come together to create a more successful future.

I moved my workstation back on to the main floor and began contributing as much as I could. I hustled, made sales calls, and did whatever I thought was needed. This move wasn't warmly embraced at the beginning, but over time, they began to trust me again.

They saw that I was being honest with them, that I was actually walking the talk. Although it took time, effort, and a little creativity to get there, everyone knew we were under new management.

VALUE CLARIFICATION

After resetting our culture, saying goodbye to our president, and getting back to basics, we all agreed it was time to take stock of our values. We had previously paid lip service to identifying core values of the company, but they weren't representative of a healthy culture. For example, some values such as "respect" and "professionalism" might look good on paper, but when they were verbally spoken, they felt passive-aggressive. We had spent the past several months realigning as a group, and I wanted a new set of values to reflect that status.

As entrepreneurs, we are, for the most part, more hardwired to be doers rather than planners, especially when it comes to identifying company values. But that doesn't diminish the importance of the process and understanding how it may contribute to team building, team confidence, and team collaboration—the cornerstones of a successful company.

Our new core values creation process meant getting feedback from the team on how everyone perceived the company. Since we wanted it to be anonymous and nonthreatening to encourage more participation, we asked team members to do the following:

1. Write down on a piece of paper one word that describes the company and our culture, and place it in the large clear bowl on the boardroom table.
2. Please add as many words as you like.
3. At the end of the month, the leadership team will collect the value words and narrow them down.
4. The prioritized list will be presented to the entire staff for feedback in the selection of five key values for the company.

The response was amazing; we had over one hundred brightly coloured pieces of paper in the bowl, and it looked really exciting. I invited my leadership team to my house for cocktails and a brainstorming session. We were blown away by the quality of the responses. We narrowed the words down to twenty from the initial hundred and presented those to all staff members for their input. We finally were able to identify our company's five values:

VALUE #1: GROWTH MINDSET

Everyone working together with an underlying interest and motivation to enhance company and individual opportunities for growth and sustainability.

VALUE #2: FUN

Providing an atmosphere that welcomes and promotes the concept of having fun as a means for increased communication, connectedness, and collaboration.

VALUE #3: ABOVE AND BEYOND

Going the extra mile to deliver successful results for our clients and candidates, reaching or surpassing the company's goals and objectives for the year, and being the best we can be as a company and as individuals.

VALUE #4: ACCOUNTABILITY

Recognizing the company is only as good as the people within it, and how important it is for everyone to accept accountability for its shortcomings and successes.

VALUE #5: HEART

The heart is our most important organ, and it is perhaps the most important quality within an organization, as it provides the drive to achieve goals, the empathy to encourage others to carry on when the going gets tough, and the cohesive bonds to ensure no team member is left behind.

It is important to keep in mind; we are talking about our values, not goals and objectives. As time and circumstances change, you should modify your values to ensure you are keeping pace with the world in which you live and your evolving business. Each time we go through the process, there is a renewed commitment and expanded sense of belonging. Try it; you'll like it!

CORE VALUES IMPLEMENTATION

The big question that evolved from our interest and desire to establish our new core values was: how do I implement them? The purpose was to identify values that would be prevalent and actionable within the company on a day-to-day basis to the point where an outsider wouldn't have to ask what our values were; they would see them in action. I quickly learned this would be a much greater challenge than I originally expected, and then the idea was born to establish a rhythm of acknowledging colleagues for living our values by giving them a shout-out.

The idea went like this: At the end of our company meetings, we would take some time to give each other "core value shout-outs." Every employee was given a set of beautiful little cards they could fill out, bring to the staff meeting, and hand out to the person they wanted to acknowledge after sharing the specific experience and value they lived.

Participation wasn't mandatory, and it wasn't quickly embraced, either! For a while—for a long, long while, I was the only person who actually handed out any shout-out cards.

I couldn't blame my team members for being hesitant about the whole experiment. They had every reason to assume this was just another silly idea that would fizzle out eventually. But as uncomfortable as it made me feel, I showed up to every meeting with a handful of shout-outs, which I would then make a big show of pinning on our bulletin board.

Eventually, a few team members showed up with their own shout-out cards, then at the next meeting, there were a few more, and then a few more. Eventually, after eighteen months of persistence, the agenda item that took up the least amount of time at every meeting became the highlight of the meeting.

The eight-by-four-foot bulletin board swelled with shout-outs—to the point where we couldn't add any new cards. They were so thickly overlaid, our pins would break as soon as we tried to push them into the board!

We stopped using the cards, but the spirit of the shout-outs still lives on. These days, we don't wait to give shout-outs at meetings; we dole them out liberally every day. Wednesday town halls are full of shout-outs, and we have dedicated a Slack channel to be used specifically for daily praise to individuals. In case you haven't used it yet, Slack is essentially a chat room for your whole company, designed to replace email as your primary method of communication and sharing. In addition to using it for projects and collaboration, we have found it to be a great tool for team communication and shout-outs. Such as:

"You crushed it today!"

"You played an integral role in us winning the business."

"Thanks for going and doing volunteer work with me tonight."

"Today marks your fifth anniversary. Thanks for being part of Creative Niche and for your incredible contribution to our growth over the last year!"

Shout-outs have become an integral part of our culture—and it's been a magical process to watch.

At the end of the day, people want to be acknowledged. Your job is to facilitate that conversation by creating an environment where everyone is encouraged to join in and actively participate. The implementation of our core values didn't just transform our culture; it impacted all of our lives. Everyone became so strong, so aligned, and so energized that productivity soared. It felt like those early, high-growth years all over again where enthusiasm and positive vibes prevailed. Everyone knew how to be successful. They were killing it, celebrating everyone's wins, and having a lot of fun in the process.

Perhaps the most unexpected outcome was the increased insight it provided to me as company leader of the individual performance and attitude behaviours of my team. When a particular person is consistently earning shout-outs, it is a definite indicator they may be a top performer. From that initial perspective, you have an easy context with which to start a conversation about a salary increase, additional responsibilities, or even a title change.

Instead of waiting for an employee to approach you to ask for a raise, you can be proactive by approaching them. Aside from it being the right and best thing to do, what a great tool it is for attracting and retaining new hires!

On the flip side, you'll also see who *isn't* standing out. This can be a red flag, but be careful. Just because a person isn't getting shout-outs doesn't mean they are a bad fit or problematic. If someone isn't getting any shout-outs, it's important to investigate why that isn't happening. It could be they are getting lost in the shuffle of a large team or, if in a more junior position, not directly impacting individuals. In that case, it may be important to examine your values to ensure they are applicable to both the business and the team.

Conversely, it could mean a person who isn't being acknowledged really isn't contributing to your values, your culture, or your business. Open up a dialogue with that individual. Try to discover whether they feel truly aligned with your values and their role within the company. Whatever the feelings are, bring them to the surface for closer examination. Chances are, they are also aware they aren't getting any shout-outs and are ready to talk to someone about it. Whatever the circumstances, if changes are required, be prepared to make them. As I learned the hard way, not taking action was a detractor to my company's culture and my role as leader.

MAKING FUN THE NORM

Leaving an established and secure job with benefits, opportunities for advancement, and retirement funding to pursue entrepreneurship seems crazy to most people. But what entrepreneurs do have is flexibility, freedom, and creativity in decision-making, developing new products and services, and changing their business. I wanted to leverage that creativity and flexibility in creating a culture where people felt trusted and trusting, offering unique perks and experiences, along with a greater sense of connectedness to our success.

But, more than anything, I wanted to have fun at work.

I am a silly, fun person, but over the past few years, the fun at the office had disappeared. Of course, I couldn't just mandate that people begin having fun. I had to create that environment.

My team was primarily composed of women, and most of them had never played foosball. They didn't know what they were missing. I picked up a table, set it up in the office, and issued a challenge to one and all to try and beat me. Five years and thousands of games later, we play foosball most days, but now it is very aggressive—I've turned all these wonderful people into monsters! We even have a big whiteboard that gets updated daily with scores!

Wanting to take things further, I formed a committee to be in charge of organizing fun things to do and special events. We established a weekly budget for the committee to create random acts of fun, a happy hour, or anything else they could think of that would create a fun experience for everyone. I also put aside funds for a big-money budget to cover the cost of events, such as our annual ski trip and summer getaway.

In 2014, I declared that every day from 2:30 to 3:00 p.m. was mandatory screen-free time—and that included cell phones.

The team wasn't productive from 2:30 to 3:00 p.m. anyway,

including me. I figured if we weren't getting anything done, we might as well use that time to take a nap, go for a walk, play foosball, or do some stretching. We have a really nice office space—I wanted the team to use it! We haven't looked back, and neither have our results. It's amazing how much we have been able to achieve during the time from three to five.

WHAT KEEPS YOU UP AT NIGHT?

From my association with many other individuals in business, I have concluded there are two worries that keep entrepreneurs up at night: money and people.

In my case, it was people. For a while, I was the ringmaster of a pretty dysfunctional culture. Even though my team members weren't bad people, many had become jaded. For some, it happened before they joined the company, but there were others who had become jaded after they started working with me.

Regardless of how it happened, the period from 2012 to 2013 was a dark time for Creative Niche. It was some of the hardest work I've ever had to do—even harder than riding out the Great Recession—but, we got through it. Eventually, I was able to salvage my relationship with my company, with my team, and with my brand. What a transformative journey.

You never quite know how toxic your environment may have become until you delve into it with the purpose of creating change. The drama, the disrespect, and the passive-aggressive attacks all combined to make me feel unwelcome in my own company. To be fair, much of that negativity was earned, and I knew that if I was going to change the culture, I had to change myself first.

I was lucky to look in the mirror and get my shit together just in time.

As a result, in just one year, I was able to transform myself and my company into the amazing workplace I always knew it could be. I'd never wish my struggles on anyone, but having experienced it helped me to find myself again—and enabled me to fall back in love with both my business and my role as leader.

Once again, I had purpose and confidence. I was ready to explore exciting new opportunities. But after all I'd been through, I never imagined what I might be getting myself into!

CHAPTER 10

PARTNERSHIPS, INVESTMENT, AND NEW HORIZONS

RED ACADEMY

It had been thirteen years since I started my company, and I had been in the same industry for seventeen years. I had grown significantly through my trials and tribulations and was continuing to learn and evolve, but I was also itching for a new challenge.

My path had intersected with the education world quite a bit. I sat on several curriculum advisories for colleges. I gave presentations at schools and critiqued students' work, and I interviewed more than 2,000 people in the industry. As a recruiter, I've spent years gaining insights from leaders and hiring managers on what they felt were gaps in the educational system as it related to producing employable tech and design talent.

From my unique vantage point, it boiled down to a pipeline problem. The education institutions weren't enabling students to acquire the skills the industry was demanding. Part of the problem was curriculum-based, while the other part was the university structure and format. So much of the professional knowledge in the industry is gained through applied learning or learning by doing, just as skills have been acquired for hundreds of years through apprenticeships with tradespeople in every sector of society. This process is the exact opposite of what most universities provide.

Even a casual look into the future indicated the opportunities to provide focused training were going to expand exponentially. Not only did the next generation of graduates need supplementary training, the existing population needed new skills in order to secure employment.

So, when I met my soon-to-be co-founder, a fellow entrepreneur who saw the same problems in education that I did, we decided to go into business together. We founded RED (Real Education and Development) Academy, a leading-edge tech and design college for the designers, creators, developers, and digital marketers of tomorrow. We saw RED as being a radical change agent in education.

Things moved quickly. We met in February, and in April, we signed our shareholder agreement, which led to a whirlwind of activity—developing curriculum, setting up and furnishing our first campus, building our brand, developing our marketing strategy, and putting our core startup team in place.

From that early momentum, we were able to open our second campus in Toronto only six months after Vancouver, and then London, England, seven months later. In just eighteen months, RED had become an international force to be reckoned with in the professional education world.

THE RED METHOD

In creating this design, we also saw an opportunity to create a real-world impact. At RED Academy, we wanted our students to acquire the necessary skills right away, so they could be employable upon graduation. From day one, students participated in an accelerated learning environment. They worked on real projects with nonprofit organizations and charities to gain the experience they could brag about on their resumes. They learned about personality styles, personal development, how to give and receive feedback, and how to work cross-discipline, all within an agency-style environment.

Through this approach, RED Academy became one of the

highest-ranked colleges of its kind on the international stage. In addition, we achieved $5 million in pro bono work for nonprofits and impacted numerous organizations and tech startups in our first four years of operation.

What I'm truly proud of is that 90 percent of the 2,000+ graduates were hired within six months of completing the program. It was an honour and a privilege to be a part of something that has transformed so many lives.

Of course, none of this would have been possible without our amazing staff. From the outset, we knew that if we were going to create an interactive learning environment with a cutting edge curriculum, we needed amazing instructors with intrapreneurial mindsets to anchor and enrich the experience.

NEW LEARNING CURVES

RED Academy has been a very different experience from founding Creative Niche. First, it was my second company, so I had a little bit of experience under my belt to draw from. Second, my role was primarily as investor and advisor; I wasn't regularly involved in the day-to-day running of the company. Third, we had a lot of millennials on our team, which injected new energy into the process. Fourth, we had to learn a lot—and quickly—without any government funding or support. We had to go through the accreditation process, build curriculum, come up with the teaching methodology, and then hire and grow quickly.

Finally, there is a lot of complexity in the education sector, and since we came from a professional services background, we had to learn how to navigate this new world, build a world-class curriculum and team, and then overcome the standard startup struggles. Honestly, I may have had more sleepless nights in a couple of years with RED Academy than I did during the entire first decade at Creative Niche—and that's counting the recession!

On more than one occasion during the first few years, I thought, "What have I done? My life was so good! If I hadn't co-founded RED, I could have taken a step back to enjoy my life." But I didn't, and once again, I found myself worrying about payroll, surprise resignations, and hiring to fuel our growth. For a while, it felt like every day I was being questioned as per the following:

> *"Hey, Mandy. Can you deposit a hundred grand in the bank tomorrow to make payroll?"*

> *"Mandy, we may lose our accreditation and have to shut down a campus."*

> *"Hey Mandy, I don't want to bother you, but we only have forty grand in the bank."*

Our burn rate was out of control. In the early days, it felt like we were hemorrhaging cash. Our investors kept backing out at the last minute, which meant I had to fill the gap. There were times I worried that each coming week might be our last.

NO REGRETS

From day one, my co-founder and I were both all-in, no looking back, no hesitation. We were very committed.

Sure, there are things both of us would have done differently, but I wouldn't have wanted to miss the opportunity, as I learned so much during the process. Just as I did when I put in the time to get Creative Niche to a stable place, those early years with RED Academy provided me with an incredible learning experience.

In saying that, what made it all possible was the fact that Creative Niche was in good hands with the team structure I had put in place. It allowed me to free myself to invest my time, energy, and money into the first two years of RED's life. It worked. I had helped build a healthy, thriving business that has impacted thousands of lives. It was time to breathe a sigh of relief—at least, so I thought.

WHEN IT RAINS, IT POURS

After fifteen years, my marriage came to an end. We had tried therapy, but it didn't take long for it to become clear that the gap between us was nearly impossible to bridge, and we made the hard decision to go our separate ways. I packed up my stuff, piled the kids and dog into my car, and then left to go and set up a new house.

Right around the same time, my other sister, who lived in Salt Lake City, Utah, was diagnosed with stage-four cancer on her fiftieth birthday. After a few rough months of treatment, I got the call that the cancer was too advanced. The chemo was killing her, and she had decided to live out the rest of her days in peace. From that point on, every moment I could muster up, I would be on the phone with her or by her side in Salt Lake. It was a struggle to get through those months, but I was managing as best as I could.

I was having dinner with my kids in the backyard on a Sunday evening when I started getting text messages from the leadership team at RED Academy, the backbone of the company. Without them, the whole business would collapse, and right now, they were all threatening to walk. I had twelve hours to fix it.

According to the team leader, the issue centred around interpersonal communications with my co-founder. I'd had no problem confronting the issue previously, but with what had been going on in my life, I hadn't been able to attend and act as a referee at every meeting. Unfortunately, communication had become more toxic when I wasn't around, and the leadership team had finally reached a breaking point. I almost had as well.

Rather than fly to Vancouver to resolve the situation in person, I called an advisor and my co-founder for an emergency meeting. I explained that the leadership team was going to quit because of the hostile work environment. I suggested that I fill in as CEO for the next six months so he could take a step back to relax and reevaluate. Afterwards, he could reenter his role, or we could find another CEO.

Beginning in May, I ran both RED Academy and Creative Niche as I split my time between Toronto and Vancouver, with side trips to Salt Lake City to comfort my sister. She passed in August, and I soldiered on until October, when I handed the leadership reins back to my partner. I was spent and couldn't do it anymore.

Although the culture had stabilized, it continued to struggle. Still, he shielded himself somewhat from the reality of the situation and continued to manage with the same leadership style that had created the problems in the first place.

I and others knew that we had been part of something incredible. I couldn't have been prouder of our team and the company, but at that point in my life, my only option was to resign from the board and extract myself from the day-to-day operations of the company.

I have no regrets. I'd never taken on a partner before, but I went in with my eyes wide open, knowing that not every partnership has a happy ending. That's just part of being in business.

I *had* done my due diligence and followed the advice of my lawyer when he said: "You need to think about your divorce before you think about your marriage." In other words, when you are creating a partnership or looking into investor opportunities, you need to understand your options when an irreconcilable difference raises its ugly head. What does it mean legally? What does it mean from a responsibility standpoint? How will it impact communication? How do you get your investment back into your bank account?

However, it is a moot point today, as COVID-19 appears to have struck a final blow against the company. RED Academy ceased operations in April 2020.

As the saying goes, "Tis better to have tried and failed than to have never tried at all."

CONCLUSION

Building a business the right way isn't easy. In fact, it's a lot of hard work—and the outcome is far from guaranteed.

If you're going to be an entrepreneur, you have to learn how to ride out the ebbs and the flows, the highs and the lows. Sometimes you will feel defeated and unable to continue. Sometimes you'll feel like you never belonged in this world in the first place. Sometimes it really is all you can do to call in sick, curl up in a ball on your couch, and wish you'd chosen a normal life.

But remember this: you're not alone.

When you're on the bottom, you will rise again. How do I know? Because you're an entrepreneur. Because you've chosen the hard path. Because you dared to look at your life and expect something more.

For those reasons alone, I know that you are resilient. I know that you are stronger than you think. I know that, even when you're at your lowest point, there are people out there who will gladly reach down, offer a helping hand, and help pull you back on top.

YOU'VE GOT THIS

I wish I could say that by reading this book, you'll be able to magically avoid all the tough times that come with entrepreneurship. But tough times are just part of the deal. When they do roll around, here are a few things to remember.

First, don't beat yourself up. Now is not the time to feel ashamed, resentful, or even regretful. Now is the time to focus, to roll up your sleeves, to get the right people in place to help you, and to turn things around.

Second, celebrate the highs. Enjoy yourself when things are going well. You will need to draw on that feeling when times are low.

Third, celebrate the lows. Your life and your career are a journey. Some of the most valuable lessons are hard-earned. You can avoid some of it, but not all of it. Besides, life would be boring if everything was flat all the time. To enjoy the adventure of entrepreneurship, you must be ready to meet both the good and the bad head-on.

TAKE THAT STEP

Hopefully, after reading this book, you have a few new ideas for getting yourself unstuck. Even during the most challenging periods of my business, even when we had lost all forward momentum completely, I was always sure there was a path forward. *I've made it this far*, I'd tell myself, *so why not take things a little further?*

If there's one big takeaway from my experiences, it's that finding the path forward often means taking a step back. Perhaps there is something you're missing, some aspect of your business that isn't running as it should—but that could once again with a little bit of creativity.

Sometimes, you might even need to step way back, all the way back to the beginning. Maybe you need to reconsider your business model, your strategic positioning in the market, or how you structure your workforce and empower them to succeed. Maybe you need to finally make the changes that you haven't wanted to face. Maybe you just need to remember why you started this business in the first place so you can fall in love with it all over again.

Whatever the case may be, the only way to move forward, the only way to rebuild your confidence, is to take that first step.

Every time I fell out of love with my business, stepping back allowed me to find my fire once again. I was able to get a new perspective on my problems, make some changes, and reengage. Again, it wasn't easy, but it was the right thing to do. I owed it to myself, I owed it to my employees, and I owed it to my business to at least go down swinging. Luckily, it never came to that—we always found a way to keep from sliding past the point of no return.

Sometimes, I'm amazed we were able to pull through. There were days, weeks, even months where I was deeply unhappy, when all I wanted to do was clear my schedule, turn on Netflix, and ignore the rest of the world. That's natural—some days, you're going to feel that way too. But rather than let those moments defeat you, use them as a turning point, an opportunity to rest, recharge, and light a fire underneath you.

ARE YOU IN LOVE WITH YOUR BUSINESS?

Before you put down this book and head off to change the world, I want you to ask yourself one last question:

Are you in love with your business?

Remember why you signed up to be an entrepreneur: to have freedom, to make money, to enjoy yourself, to make a difference—to have something that's uniquely yours, something that you're proud of.

If you're not in love, then why not? What is standing in the way of you and happiness, and what is the first step you can take to get back to where you're feeling engaged and excited again? Are you not making enough money? Have you lost the confidence of your team? Are you losing confidence in your product?

Whatever the problem might be, your first step is to identify it.

Then, your next step is to start designing the business that you love.

So what are you waiting for? Let's get to it.

ACKNOWLEDGMENTS

This book wouldn't have been possible without:

The unconditional love and unwavering support from incredible family and loved ones.

The help and inspiration I received from friends, advisors, mentors, and fellow entrepreneurs.

My team, who stuck by me and made me a better leader and entrepreneur.

Clients and leaders who took a chance on me.

My dad, Chas Hoppe, and the Scribe Tribe, who helped me tell my story.

ABOUT THE AUTHOR

MANDY GILBERT is an entrepreneur, CEO, investor, and speaker. In 2002, she started Creative Niche, a recruitment firm specializing in advertising, digital, and marketing, with $8,000. Today, it brings in nearly $12 million in sales and has placed thousands of creative, digital, and marketing talent across North America. Mandy has been recognized as a United Nations Global Accelerator and completed the EO/ MIT Entrepreneurial Masters Program. She lives in Toronto and is the proud mom of two busy boys, Isaac and Sam. Mandy is a weekly columnist for *Inc*.

Made in the USA
Monee, IL
30 January 2021